PRAISE FOR *THE CHAPO GUIDE TO REVOLUTION*

"I haven't had my worldview exploded by a political work like this since reading *Millie's Book* in 1992."

—Patton Oswalt, *New York Times* bestselling author of *Silver Screen Fiend*

"The raucous dirtbag hilarity of the Chapo crew sometimes masks the fact that they reliably provide some of the most incisive, sophisticated, and thought-provoking political analysis found on any platform. Their book is as intellectually serious and analytically original as it is irreverent and funny, and it deserves substantial discussion and all of the gushing and angry reactions it will inevitably provoke."

—Glenn Greenwald, *New York Times* bestselling author of *No Place to Hide*

"In my day, it didn't take fifteen goddamn people to write a book. Nevertheless, this was an exceptional, funny, and entertaining read. Howard Zinn on acid or some bullshit like that."

—Tim Heidecker, coauthor of *Tim and Eric's Zone Theory*

"Garrote sharp, acerbic, smart, inventive, and truly laugh-out-loud funny, *The Chapo Guide to Revolution* feels like it was written by the offspring of the shotgun marriage of *The Onion,* Howard Zinn, Dorothy Parker, Bill Hicks, Noam Chomsky, and Jonathan Swift. If they all got together and fucked and had one baby, I mean. I LOVED this book."

—David Cross, *New York Times* bestselling author of *I Drink for a Reason*

"Perhaps in Victorian England a spoonful of sugar helped the medicine go down, but in the hellscape of contemporary American politics, the Chapo Trap House crew does well to swap out sweetener and deliver its punchy political analysis with a big dose of snark, wit, and lolz. Lovers of the podcast will revel in righteous takedowns and scathing portraits of galling political self-interest, while newcomers to the brand and veterans alike will enjoy the frank and funny introduction to the contemptible political players, online feuds, Marxist themes, and partisan blood-letting that are the grist of the Chapo podcast, and which have made it a site of catharsis for an entire doomed generation."

—Briahna Joy Gray, senior politics editor at *The Intercept*

"Finally a book that explains why I shouldn't like Matt Yglesias. And so many others. All the monsters we encounter online have been laid out and torn asunder in spectacular fashion. This book is like those fleeting moments of the Chapo Trap House podcast that have clarity."

—Dave Anthony, coauthor of *The United States of Absurdity*

PRAISE FOR CHAPO TRAP HOUSE

"Intolerant Vulgarians."

—The Federalist

"Aggressively masculine."

—Jamie Kirchick

"Juvenile guys with one lady who trash people and talk about obscure and sometimes gross topics."

—Joan Walsh

"Conveys a hunger for dominance and submission."

—The New Republic

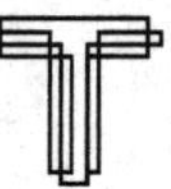

THE CHAPO

to

REVOL

GUIDE

A Manifesto Against Logic, Facts, and Reason

UTION

CHAPO TRAP HOUSE

Felix Biederman, Matt Christman, Brendan James,
Will Menaker, and Virgil Texas

Art by ELI VALLEY and JON WHITE

TOUCHSTONE
New York London Toronto Sydney New Delhi

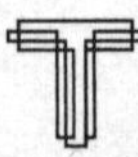

Touchstone
An Imprint of Simon & Schuster, Inc.
1230 Avenue of the Americas
New York, NY 10020

First Touchstone hardcover edition August 2018

Interior design by Jason Snyder

Manufactured in the United States of America

10 9 8 7 6 5 4

Library of Congress Cataloging-in-Publication Data is available.

ISBN 978-1-5011-8728-5
ISBN 978-1-5011-8730-8 (ebook)

This book is dedicated to the brave Mujahideen fighters of Afghanistan.

CONTENTS

INTRODUCTION

BORROW THIS BOOK

*or two years now, you've been asking, "Who is Chapo Trap House?" This is Chapo Trap House speaking. We are Chapo, a podcast that loves life, coffee, doggos, bourbon, and intelligent debate. We are the podcast that does not sacrifice our love for those things or our values. We are the ironic pieces of shit who have deprived you of victims and thus destroyed your world with your own logic. If you wish to know why you're perishing—you who dread knowledge—we are the gang who will now tell you.*

If you're reading these words, you're likely living in despair and hopelessness. You're fed a steady diet of thin, flavorless gruel by your leaders, your parents, fake friends who love drama, the fascist mods on Erowid and r/celebritytoes, the lying sheeple news media, and, most especially, all previous works of political satire and comedy. You find yourself in the dumbest of all possible worlds, clowns to the left of you, *Re-thug-licans* to the right. And the president? How about . . . NO. Like a veal calf, you sit in your crate, every day growing sadder, softer, and more delicious, thinking, *There's got to be a better way!*

Friend, we're here to tell you that there *is* a better way: the Chapo Way.

This is the beginning of a journey you will never forget. In this book, we'll survey the blasted landscape of contemporary American politics and culture through our scientific ideology of irony, half-baked Marxism, revolutionary discipline, NoFap November, and posting on the Internet. You'll become an initiate in the Chapo Mindset and take control of the neurons that govern your weak, fragile emotions. You will experience success, probably for the first time. You will learn to live *your* life on *your* terms. By buying this book and all its affiliated content, you'll improve your health and fitness, have stronger relationships, straighten your posture, purify your brain chemistry, and gain more focus. Your children and ex-wife *will* respect you.

In addition to desiring to become a Brain-Clear Alpha Silverback Gray Wolf, you're probably also interested in politics, and in taking a sideways glance at the news through the lens of satire. Maybe you became politically aware one crisp, clear Tuesday morning in September, when you got the day off from school; you noticed your local GameStop clerk had tears in his eyes as he waived your late fee on *Tom Clancy's Rainbow Six*. Perhaps around the time America decided to invade Afghanistan and then Iraq, you had an inkling that living in the End of History wasn't going to be as utopian as promised. Maybe after John Kerry reported for duty at the 2004 Democratic Convention, you felt a brief twinge of patriotic embarrassment followed by a bone-deep sense that things will never get better. Or maybe it was when you graduated from college with six figures of debt around the time the economy shit its insides out.

It's possible you briefly lost that feeling of impending doom in 2008, after the likable, cool presidential candidate defeated the old man who slept through all his flight school classes. But that relief probably vanished in a wave of Wall Street bailouts and drone strikes and a brief Democratic congressional majority that didn't even bother to pass the card check bill or push for true universal health care. Perhaps once you got a job, you realized that the pay—or, if you were really lucky, the benefits package—was vastly outweighed by what work took out of your soul, as you spent your days white-knuckling it from check to check, feeling like the same idiot failure you were before you had a job. In any case, the last presidential election probably left you completely lost, tossed about in the gaping maw of twenty-first-century America. You're just another plastic bag adrift in the ocean with no power, no future, and not even a symbolic say in politics.

More bad news: since 2016, the Democratic Party—the standard-bearer of left-of-center policies like replacing unions with low-interest Uber loans and bringing charter-school apps to Haiti—has stopped even pretending to fight for you.

All this leaves a new power vacuum on the left, in which we have taken up residence. The mummies in the Democratic Party are busy trying to rebrand Clintonesque bromides like "entrepreneurship" and "education reform," while the average, young working person is desperate for health care, free college, and a steady job that pays them in something other than Applebee's Lunch Combo coupons.

Our case is simple: Capitalism, and the politics it spawns, is not working for anyone under thirty who is not a sociopath. It's not supposed to. The actual lived experience of the free market feels distinctly un-free. We'll tell you why, and offer a vision of a new world—one in which a person can post in the morning, game in the afternoon, and podcast after dinner without ever becoming a poster, gamer, or podcaster.

Bernie Sanders's unexpected victories in the 2016 primaries and Jeremy Corbyn's Labour Party's near-upset nearly a year later revealed the false choice between the Democrats' bloodless liberalism and the lizard-brained right wing. You don't have to side with either the pear-shaped vampires of the Right *or* the craven, lanyard-wearing corporate wonks of the center-left. Dark days lie ahead, and many people are finally hungry for a fully ironic ideology for no-good, entitled, downwardly mobile, politically hopeless millennials.

More than anything, though, the current situation demands a huge expansion of what is considered "realistic" or possible.

No, Seriously, Who Are You?

We are posters. We earn what we get in trade for what we post. We ask for nothing more or less than what we post. That is justice.

What you call *Chapo Trap House* began as the brainchild of three chums who met on Twitter. In early 2016, Felix Biederman, Matt Christman, and Will Menaker sought a platform to discuss the upcoming election and also bring awareness to the disturbing presence of Dyson Airblades in most public restrooms (did you know they actually spread 1,300 times more bacteria than simple paper towels?). Soon after, Brendan James, Virgil Texas, and Amber A'Lee Frost came aboard, and despite the obvious lack of production value or the faintest tinge of professionalism, *Chapo* soon became a hit among dog fanciers, garnering profiles in prestigious old media outlets like the *New York Gentleman, New York Place, Manhattan Times*, the *Knickerbocker*, and *Feet & Stream*. Since then, our humble gabfest has become a Lovecraftian language-virus boring tunnels through the brains of all who encounter us.

The important thing to remember is that, no matter who we

are or where we came from, we invented leftism in America and are the only real socialists. If you encounter someone claiming otherwise, they're a Hitlerian-NATO-stalking-horse running dog. Please record their name, address, and any other relevant details and send it c/o Chapo Emergency Commission for Combating Counterrevolution and Sabotage, PO Box 420-69, Penn Station, New York, NY 10001.

In order to guard against those kinds of revisionists, it's important to inculcate you, the reader, with the correct manifesto mindset. After you cut ties with your family and all your aforementioned fake friends, you'll be prepared to properly imbibe the lessons we're about to teach you. Go do that.

Now, you may be asking yourself, *Chapo, once you seize power, what will the country look like? Will all my favorite stories still be on the television?* Yes—however, you may notice a few changes when you're living in Year Zero of our Utopia. The political program exists as follows:

1. Three-day workweek, four-hour workday.
2. Health care, childcare, education, housing, and food are free and paid for by turning all existing billionaires into thousandaires and/or Soylent.
3. The use of logic, facts, and reason is outlawed.
4. Feelings become fiat currency.

5. The police are replaced by robot cops of some kind.

6. Everyone gets a dog

7. All drugs are legalized and also become safe, healthy, and nonaddictive.

8. Every single person involved in creating, promoting, and planning the Iraq War is pushed into a volcano.

9. Control of all media, newspapers, journalism, etc., is turned over to a mysterious Big Brother–style figure known only as "The Beer Nerd."

10. Official state religion is Shia Scientology.

Things to Come . . .

In the chapters that follow, we'll act as Virgil Texas to your Dante on a tour of the hell-realm of politics and culture.

To kick things off in chapter one, we'll explain in a hasty and tossed-off manner the creation of the modern geopolitical scene. We'll analyze the nature and motivations of every major player on the global stage, based on only slightly outdated psychological profiles and phrenology. For example, in Russia, we see the incubator of the global right wing, which hacked America's election by installing Hillary Clinton as the 2016 Democratic nominee. In friendly France, we see a proud Enlightenment tradition that cherishes democracy and free expression, primarily through the medium of obscene, phallus-based political cartoons. The world is indeed complex, and is therefore boring—so we'll do our best to give you the information you need to craft global solutions for a global world.

In chapter two, we'll examine the history and personality of the American lib. Everyone loves a liberal, or so they tell themselves. Despite their practical cultural hegemony in movies, TV, and academia, liberals have an uncanny knack for losing elections and being generally loathed. This is in spite of their strong record of liking ethnic food, bombing ethnic countries, privatizing education, and gutting welfare. This collection of punching bags and pratfall artists whose only principle is not being Republican have somehow fallen out of favor, despite being right about everything.

How did this happen? Until the 1950s, the Communist Party had nearly succeeded in infiltrating the top levels of government, before Alger Hiss accidentally announced "I'm a Soviet spy" during his son's Bring Your Dad to School Day. His unforced error triggered a purge that threw American radicals back into opposition through the 1960s, when they won some important victories for the civil rights and antiwar movements. They also scored several less important victories, like mainstreaming vegetarianism and inventing the blazer-with-jeans look.

The 1970s produced only disappointment, from the breakdown of labor power to the incompetent McGovern campaign to the crypto-conservative-Evangelical presidency of Jimmy Carter. After Reagan primed the pump for the final stage of dystopia (amping up the war on drugs, sanitizing racial resentment, and perforating the last vestige of American union muscle), Bill Clinton rode into office and finished the job by passing welfare reform and a draconian crime bill, eviscerating consumer protections, and transferring huge amounts of political power to the superwealthy—all the while posing as a bleeding-heart pinko. In fact, Clinton *would* have privatized Social Security and gotten away with it, were it not for a certain meddling intern.

That left us with the current incarnation of the Democratic Party: pro-war, pro–Wall Street, and pro-markets. In other words, despite their tepid and always negotiable commitment to abortion, gay rights, and prestige TV, they're as right-wing as any political party should be allowed to be in the twenty-first century. The fact that they're supposed to be decent people's only form of political representation is proof enough that we're living in hell.

Is it any wonder that *liberalism* has become a dirty word, and that the task of bringing socialism back has fallen to goofies like us?

In the ongoing family-court drama that is our politics, true patriots would cast the American lib as the scheming, greedy wife who, with the aid of anti-father laws and unelected judges, takes all the money and runs off with the scuba instructor (Europe) while the children (democracy, freedom, and liberty) suffer from neglect and slide into dissolution and juvenile delinquency (socialism). Who will stand for love, family, and what we once had on our wedding night all the way back in 1776? Who will stand athwart history and scream, "STOP TURNING THE KIDS AGAINST ME!"? That lone hero is the subject of chapter three: the American conservative, or right-winger, who will fight for family and stand for what's right, even if it's "uncool," "unfashionable," or "chattel slavery."

In chapter four, we shoot the messenger: the media, who, in this torturous family-court analogy, was friends with both liberals *and* conservatives in college before getting married and eventually divorced and wants to remain friends with *both* parties. The media is the guardian of discourse, and in the future, the only media that will exist will, of course, be *Chapo* and *Chapo*-approved affiliates. We'll focus entirely on liquidating the "legitimate news" part of the media, along with its revolting acolytes, known as "journalists." In this chapter, however, we'll provide a history of the prerevolutionary news media, from the early days of the printing press to the dawn of the blogosphere and beyond.

Of course, it was once said by the great political satirist and cocaine enthusiast Andrew Breitbart that politics is downstream from culture. We're peeing in the same gutter: before one can truly understand politics, one has to watch a lot of television shows and movies—especially those aimed at children—and chapter five has you covered. In a broad survey of the dominant strains of contemporary culture, we destroy the fascist and imperialist aesthetic that rules our time. In its place, we offer you the correct cultural opinions and a slate of preapproved films, TV shows, art, and sculpture.

Finally, in chapter six, we roll up our sleeves, bring our lunch pail to the job site, and develop an opioid addiction after destroying our joints writing about how much jobs suck. From the agricultural labor that made the fertile crescent to the dark satanic content mills of today, work has always plagued humanity, sapping our energy and stealing time that could be better spent doing nothing. We'll dispense with many of the comforting myths about work that permeate our society—namely, that "small" businesses and their owners are good, that hard work is its own reward, and that education, marriage, and "skills" represent a path out of exploitation and poverty.

In addition, chapter six will also touch on the most dynamic and exciting part of our economy and, therefore, our politics: technology. It's the engine that drives innovation and disrupts all the old ways of being human. The tech industry has changed how we work, date, eat, and not have sex in the few hours between. But as the singularity approaches, we must face certain ethical and political quandaries, such as: What do we do with the surplus population put out of work by robots—and can we fuck those robots, even if they become self-aware?

That's pretty much it. Once you read this book, you will possess the mindset to participate in the vanguard of the coming revolution. Achieving a Chapo-run society will require revolutionary discipline, but make no mistake: the world will change when you're ready to pronounce this oath:

> I swear by my life and my love of it that I will never live for the sake of another political comedy podcast, nor another shitty, neoliberal Democratic Party candidate for fear of whatever right-wing ghoul they're running against.

One last thing: If you're a fan of sacred cows, prisoners being taken, and holds being barred, then stop reading immediately. This book is *not* for you. However, if you feel alienated, dispossessed, and disenfranchised from the political and cultural nightmare that is America, then . . .

Chapo, let's go.

CHAPTER ONE

WORLD

I am a citizen of the world.

—DIOGENES

The world is a vampire.

—SMASHING PUMPKINS

ou may find it odd that we'd start a book about the American nightmare with a chapter on the rest of the world. You reveal your own ignorance. The great thing about having an empire is that no matter where you are on earth, you're home! And you can't really understand America's internal rot—its inflamed, wriggling bowels—unless you understand its role as a brutal, stupid, and self-owning empire.

But just how did America grow from a small-time, mom-and-pop plantation into a gigantic, ruthlessly efficient multinational? After some initial growing pains, the United States debuted some innovative imperial pilot programs like Cuba and Hawaii in the late nineteenth century. But it wasn't until after World War II that we truly inherited Great Britain's mantle as the international point man for capital. America would soon end up invading/sabotaging/destroying literally *most* of the countries in the world in pursuit of maximum synergy.

Hostile Makeover

The US emerged from World War II as the Chad of nations. (The Nation of Chad did not come into existence until 1960.) Our rival Nazi Germany had collapsed after it overleveraged risky investments in Eastern European "living space," while Japan—once an aggressive competitor to America—was defeated due to a certain killer app developed in a cutting-edge incubator in Los Alamos, New Mexico. Not only were our enemies out of the game, but our British, French, and Dutch colleagues were all bankrupt, leaving America ready to expand our portfolio and pick up these assets from declining empires for pennies on the dollar.

To manage this sprawling enterprise, we reorganized our top talent into a streamlined corporate structure. The newly formed Defense Department was put in charge of human resources; the International Monetary Fund handled accounting, using the Bretton Woods bookkeeping system; the CIA headed up marketing, underwriting radio spots in Eastern Europe and some truly groundbreaking abstract advertisements by Mark Rothko and Jackson Pollock; and for R & D, we poached a team of bright young go-getters from a foundering competitor via Operation Paper Clip, one of the most successful headhunting projects in the pre-LinkedIn era.

Just as the modern economy consolidates hundreds or thousands of diverse firms into a handful of huge, pulsating conglomerates, America rode a wave of mergers and acquisitions to global monopoly. We got serious about vertical integration and started using our newfound economic and military muscle to close some really impressive deals in markets like Britain, West Germany, Japan, and—after deleting about a million people from the budget—Korea.

Korea was the first serious PowerPoint presentation of the Cold War, a showdown between us and the oppressive regulatory apparatus known as the Soviet Union. It was where we first proved our commitment to the two principles of our company philosophy: a) Kill civilians to maintain US hegemony, and b) Prop up dictators to maintain control of valuable territory. It's a simple process known as *subcontracting*, and it came in handy every time we needed to farm out the hard work of opening markets and killing Communists. During the Korean War, for example, Syngman Rhee was our guy; a dapper, well-dressed player who ordered thousands of extrajudicial killings and had a dick like a billy club. And long after him,

CTH WORLD FACT BOOK

This quick reference guide provides all the information you need to know about global hot spots and allies, should you visit any of these countries for business, pleasure, espionage, or to spread the message about our podcast.

TURKEY

Population: 81.5 million subscribers to our show

Top-Rated TV Show: *The Armenians' Ingratitude*, Comedy Mosque Network

Most Downloaded Apps: *Angry Kurds*, *Erdogan GO*, *Dissident Crush*

Cause of All Problems: Fethullah Gülen

US Stance: Willing to barter Gülen for national treasure Deniz, the Roundest Cat in Turkey

people tend to forget, South Korea was governed by a series of alternating military and civilian dictators. Korea set the standard: we'll do anything on behalf of anyone, especially on behalf of ourselves; that's the American promise.

So straight out of the gate, the Cold War was emphatically *not* about democracy versus totalitarianism. In Korea and in every subsequent proxy war, it was about capitalism versus threat to capitalism.

For a while, things hummed along nicely: by 1953, after the stuffy, uncreative Mohammad Mosaddeq decided to nationalize Iran's oil industry, we paid Iranian bodybuilders to help install the pro-American Shah; in 1954, we acquired Guatemala through some corporate espionage; in 1965, we handed over an electronic mailing list of known Communists to our business partner

---

SAUDI ARABIA

Population: 268 billion barrels

Top-Rated TV Show: صيادو البنات (*Daughter Auction Hunters*), Divine truTV

Political Up-and-Comers: Prince Sultan bin Faisal Abdulaziz al-Saud (age eighty-six), a bloody scimitar, a platinum-coated Lamborghini with a machine gun mounted on the hood

National Slogan: ohh lebanese sweetie i luv the feet come to riyadh i live in a castle

US Stance: Treasured ally

UNITED KINGDOM

Population: 65 million tossers

Still Has a Queen Who Rules from a Big Fancy Castle?: You bet your ass

Crime: A bloody gyppo nicked the crazy frog off me mobi whilst i was in the loo! cor blimey im joining UKIP innit

Top Exports: Buggery, High-Concept Television Programs, Pop Music Consumed by the Most Precious and Annoying Americans

US Stance: Special relationship

Indonesia, which resulted in some serious housecleaning; and also in 1965, we occupied the Dominican Republic to bail out its pro-American CEO. Inevitably, however, the day arrived when public relations took a serious hit. The problem was Vietnam, a once-promising leveraged buyout from our faltering competitor, France.

The whole thing started when the US decided to cancel a national Vietnamese election scheduled for 1956 and set up by the Geneva Accords. America saw this mess of red tape for what it was and had the South Vietnamese call it off. That, rather than whatever slogan John McCain has tattooed on his scaled thigh, is what started the entire war. At the time it seemed like a great investment. Even after assuming the previous company's liabilities (by the end of its run, America was funding about 80 percent of the French war in Indochina), these assets were going at fire-sale prices! Much like in Korea, we ended up outsourcing the

---

JAPAN

Population: 127 million tentacles

Working-Age Population: 12

Samurais: Zero since Tom Cruise

Top Exports: Girlfriend Simulators, One-Half of Comedian Dan Nainan

Top-Rated Anime: *Hi Hi Z Komodo* (small, weak teenagers must earn incredible power by fighting inside demon-powered robots), *Mister Mister* (a sickly teenager watches as superbeings of unimaginable strength face off against each other in staring contests to determine their power level), *Iron Terror Vibration* (in a postapocalyptic world, a meek but dedicated teenager must overcome his frailty to join a caste of warrior priests and fight a horde of androgynous ghosts)

US Stance: Confused, but strangely curious

management to a series of dictators: Ngo Dinh Diem, Big Minh, Nguyễn Khánh, etc. But despite our best efforts, we failed; the attempted hostile takeover killed something in the neighborhood of 3–4 million Vietnamese, and that's not even counting the spill-over in Laos and Cambodia.

7 Habits of Highly Effective Empires

It was a lesson for some, but not all, of America's board members: the ideal business relationship may not be direct, messy, bloody conflict but instead a tranquil affiliation between contractor and subcontractor, a junior who acts on the whim of the parent yet still serves its own interests in the region. Corporate should intervene only if a bigger problem arises, such as uppity trade unions demanding labor laws or casual Fridays getting out of hand. Other people drew a different lesson: every time a colonial overlord is forced by

---

BRAZIL

Population: 210 million landing strips

Economy: Kidnapping-based

Rain Forest: See it while you still can

Attitude Toward Public Toplessness: Progressive and brave

Isolated Rain Forest Tribes Who Have Still Never Heard Joe Rogan's Voice: 3

US Stance: Reciprocal friendship with right-wing coup plotters

MEXICO

Population: 130 million Breitbart articles

Our Jobs: They're takin' 'em

Drunken College Students on Spring Break Kidnapped by Drug Cartels with One Rogue Special Agent Racing against the Clock to Save Them: 7

Further Research: *Breaking Bad* season 4, episode 10, "Salud"

US Stance: Stupid, incomprehensible screaming

their declining economic standing to pull out of a country and leave a vacuum of power, that vacuum will almost certainly be filled by an anticapitalist, anti-imperialist movement.

You might be saying to yourself, *Hey, Professor Atheist Jew Libtard, put down the birth control pills and burning flag for one second and take the patriotic view: we were fighting a war to the death against Communism. If we hadn't propped up* our *dictators, wouldn't* they *have propped up* their *dictators and won?*

Here's a two-tiered answer. First, who cares? Pick your dictatorship: Would you rather have lived in Fidel Castro's Cuba or in any one of the US's many military junta police states? Second, America

---

GERMANY

Population: 82 million plump children

History: [Smiles politely, looks down at feet]

Fastest-Growing Economic Sectors: Information technology, scat pornography hygiene

National Style of Humor: Sausages in ears

Top-Rated TV Show: *Stuttgart nach München: Eine Zugfahrt!* (*Stuttgart to Munich: A Train's Journey!*), Der Aktion! Network

US Stance: Allies, with 35,000 American soldiers stationed here to defend the Munich Oktoberfest & Nude Pride Week

GREECE

Population: 11 million

Unemployed Population: 78 million

Largest Economic Sector: Licensing fees from other countries using democracy

Nice Supranational Common Market It's Got There: Be a real shame if something were to happen to it

History: The classiest of all, the progenitor of almost all the art and philosophy of the Western world, but seriously, folks, what's up with all those tiny penises on the statues? Those dicks are small. (Editor's note: *Actually*, according to every study, the penises are average- to above-average-sized.)

US Stance: Warm memories of the fascist coups we've supported

was usually targeting not just strongman regimes but democratic mass movements. And there was never a situation in which any American gain in yardage was a clear win against hegemonic Communism, because the Communist Bloc was already fragmented by the mid 1960s (not to mention the added players in the Third Way/ Non-Aligned Movement, a crunchy co-op founded by Nehru, Tito, Sukarno, Nasser, and Nkrumah).

How many times did we act not against Communism but against anything remotely subverting capitalism? United Fruit in Latin America? Iran? Democratically elected Chilean socialist Salvador Allende? In none of those cases were the Soviets to

---

FRANCE

Population: 656 million anthropomorphic candlesticks

Most Popular Professions: Racist cartoonist, cigarette tester, blackface makeup technician

Top-Grossing Movie: *L'Homme Gay Raciste* (*The Racist Gay Man*, winner of France's Jerry Lewis Award for Outstanding Satire)

Cultural Trademark: Cartoons of various local and world leaders eating poop and performing fellatio, captioned "Les Politiques"

US Stance: Frenemy

ISRAEL

Population: 8.5 million if you count the Arabs, but let's not

Government: The Middle East's only democracy, and working hard to keep it that way

Religion: Judaism and Other

History: Has existed for three thousand years in its current form

Occupied Territories: Oh my, no, you've been misinformed

Measurements: Working out every day and making gains every year

US Stance: The kindest, warmest, bravest, most wonderful ally we've ever had

be seen. (In fact, Allende was a complete pushover who decided to ignore some choice advice Castro gave him right before the coup: put guns in the hands of the workers, because they're coming to kill you. Allende's response—"No, democratic norms are important"—explains why his regime lasted a full fifteen minutes, while Fidel lived another nine hundred years.) In fact, America was

---

INDIA

Population: Hoo boy

Government: Largest fascist movement on the planet, currently hosting US secretary of state

Top Export: Other half of comedian Dan Nainan

Religion/Relationship Status: Poly

Voiced by: Hank Azaria

US Stance: Valuable global partner with bonus anti-Muslim bigotry

RUSSIA

Population: 144 million bots

Chief Exports: Tracksuits, Misery, Important Novels

Leading Cause of Death: Everything

Top-Rated TV Show: *Черт, я убил своих детей!* (*Damn, I Killed My Kids!*), Cartoon Network

US Stance: Implacable enemy

IRAN

Population: 82 million as of now, but who can say what tomorrow will bring?

Exports: Terrorism; it cannot be said enough. Iran is the world's greatest exporter of terrorism. Say it to yourself out loud right now, and say it any chance you get in the *Washington Post*, the *Atlantic*, or the *Daily Beast*, and anytime you appear on CNN.

Government: Constitutional republic subject to the veto of anyone looking stern in a framed poster

US Stance: Classic face-heel relationship

so interested in fighting the evils of Communism that it propped up *fucking Pol Pot*—AFTER the Killing Fields! Yes, the genocide in Cambodia was stopped by the Communists running North Vietnam, who drove Pol Pot out of power. But because the North Vietnamese were card-carrying Reds, America backed a Khmer Rouge comeback tour and sent SAS guys to train them in the jungles and

---

IRELAND

riverrun: past Eve and Adam's

Population: 4.7 million descendants of slaves

Exports: Charm, wit, several of the greatest novelists, poets, and playwrights of the modern era

Irish-American Exports: Police brutality, sports brutality, Boston brutality, general oafishness, petty crime

Government: A tragicomedy in two acts

Unemployment rate for unwed mothers: 0 percent

US Stance: Storage locker for Apple to stack bundles

a way: a lone a last a loved a long the

ITALY

Population: 59 million legitimate businessmen

Government: Parliamentary republic that still lives with its mother

Culture: Timeless art, screaming at women in leather skirts, being too fat to go to prison

Economy: Street harassment

Top Export: Sports cars that allow men to catcall as efficiently as possible

Most Popular TV Shows: *Bunga Bunga Party of Five* (IT4), *Hidden Camera in Senate Women's Restroom* (P-SPAN), *Top 10 Most Racist Plays of the Week* (Futbol Italia)

Top Social Media Star: Gianni Paulismo, the polite teenager who does outrageous YouTube pranks like being quiet in public, bathing, not smoking cigarettes, wearing shirts, respecting women

US Stance: Trying to correctly pronounce "prosciutto"

lay mines that are still around today and probably just atomized some poor soul as you read this paragraph. Yet Pol Pot ends up in the *Black Book of Communism.*

But such are the trade-offs inherent in running a business—and what a business we had. Funding wasn't a problem, seeing as the US was a preeminent manufacturing base, the workhouse of the free world. With the Marshall Plan and a pivot toward Asia, we were throwing cash and goods everywhere, stabilizing our postwar partners in a new global order (and securing some profits for industry, if you want to be pedantic about it). Also, with

---

KENYA

Population: 50 million accomplices to US presidential fraud

Top Export: US presidents

Chief Industries: Birth-certificate forgery

Federal Organization: 57 counties

Economy: Spreading the wealth around

Health Care: If you like your doctor, you can keep him

National Motto: You Didn't Build That

US Stance: Positive until the truth was revealed in 2009

NORWAY

Population: A horrifying sea of small tyrants who drown sensitive men in their typhoons of misery

Government: Foolish men and women who put on their suits one button at a time to pretend they don't stare at the maw of death with whatever niceties standing in their way

Economy: Mixed melancholy/command economy

Exports: Authors who write five-hundred-thousand-page autobiographies that track every argument they ever got into with their parents, Nazi occult blogs, dried fish spine

Most Popular TV Shows: My vulgar parents did not allow a television,

the Bretton Woods system that established the US dollar as the reserve currency of world trade, America entered the postwar era as the ultimate arbiter and guarantor of global capitalism. This meant that the we could afford to spend billions rebuilding the European economy (and keeping the Communists from taking power) while brokering peace between labor and capital at home. In exchange for chilling out on the worker militancy and purging Communists from any leadership positions, organized labor was promised a bigger percentage of the profits generated by America's unipolar industrial might.

---

instead wishing to fill the gaping pit of entertainment with small psychic wounds and inadequacies, *The Never-Ending Rainy Walk*, *Sir You Already Paid for Your Coffee* (top-rated comedy for the last twenty years)

Suicide Rate: 112 percent

Maximum prison sentence: Forty-five days

US Stance: Pity

CHINA

Population: 1.4 billion socialists with Chinese characteristics

Government: Under the dynamic leadership of President Xi Jinping, the full party has united in full confidence in the path, theory, and system of Chinese socialism

Economy: Socialism with Chinese characteristics is the integration of the theory of scientific socialism and the social development theories of Chinese history. This conclusion is the result of historical exploration and the will of the people.

Mao Zedong's Thought: An enduring spirit currently being upheld both in the building of the party and the advancement of the great cause of socialism with Chinese characteristics

The Rejuvenation of the Chinese Nation: A dream shared by all Chinese

National Defense: A people's armed forces that follows the Party's commands and is able to win and is exemplary in conduct

US Stance: Anxiously checking rearview mirror

Schlock Doctrine

After a half century of gridlock, we finally got the upper hand against our big governmental rival in Russia. The breakthrough came in the late 1980s after the Soviets tried to regulate small businesses in Afghanistan. Seizing the opportunity to innovate, we created a new platform for warfare that empowered independent contractors known as Mujahideen, who were looking to thrive in the gig economy. The inflexible bureaucracy of the Red Army, bogged down by licenses and worker benefits, simply couldn't compete. The beauty of our strategy lay in its simplicity: We could spend almost unlimited sums of money and create a whole slew of new jobs for self-motivated freelancers with very little screening or oversight. Sure, this led to our fair share of PR setbacks, including one-star reviews for unreliable contractors like Mohamed Atta, but that came further down the line.

EMPIRES: WHERE ARE THEY NOW?

BRITISH EMPIRE

1913

LAND AREA: 13,000,000 sq mi (approx.)

LEADER: His Majesty George V, by the Grace of God, of the United Kingdom of Great Britain and Ireland and of the British Dominions beyond the Seas, King, Defender of the Faith, Emperor of India

CAREER OPPORTUNITIES: Cannon Fodder, Sepoy, Colonial Officer Pedophile

LEADING CAUSE OF DEATH: Running straight into a hail of machine-gun fire because an inbred Etonian who looks like Nigel Thornberry ordered you to

MOTTO: The sun never sets on the British Empire

DOWNFALL: World War II

Then, in 1989, Ronald Reagan finally ended Communism by boldly declaring, "Mother, where are my jelly beans?" shitting himself, and karate-chopping the Berlin Wall exactly four times. (The combined pressures of falling oil prices, the invasion of Afghanistan, nationalist movements, and the internal contradictions of the Soviet system may also have played a role.) With collapse on the horizon, Mikhail Gorbachev was stuck with a serious crisis. Thankfully for everyone, the West was eager to lend a helping hand. This was a once-in-a-lifetime opportunity to free the East from the tyranny of planned economies and government jobs. Thanks to the ambition and corruption of Boris Yeltsin, US policymakers, and the chaos god Loki, the Soviet Union splintered into dozens of new, independent start-ups, while America and her allies carried out an aggressive strategy for the acquisition of Eastern Europe's state assets.

Yeltsin woke up on a snowmobile in 1999 with no memory

UNITED KINGDOM

2018

LAND AREA: Everything between the Tesco and the Chunnel

LEADER: Co-Emperors Noel and Liam Gallagher

CAREER OPPORTUNITIES: Hooligan, Bloke, Radio DJ Pedophile

LEADING CAUSE OF DEATH: Heart attack while posting "id give theresa a good rogering, shame corbyn wants to put her in a burka" in the *Daily Mail* comment section

MOTTO: Winter is coming

DOWNFALL: British accent no longer considered smart by rest of world

of the previous ten years. When he got back to his office in the Kremlin, his staff informed him that he'd sold off all Russia's resources to pirates, mob bosses, and Western corporate interests. (Damning, to be sure, but don't act like you haven't done worse while drunk.) Yeltsin facilitated a "shock therapy" economic liberalization program, otherwise known as private equity, assisted by American whiz kids like Jeffrey Sachs and Larry Summers. It led to the largest drop in peacetime life expectancy of the twentieth century. But they got McDonald's and Pizza Hut, so it's a wash. Why live past fifty-five when you've already fulfilled your greatest dreams?

Somehow, an epic deal like "consumer goods in exchange for the privatization of your entire economy" wasn't good enough for many Russians, and Yeltsin faced a difficult reelection campaign in 1996. A Communist Party candidate threatened to return Russia to the Bad Old Days of guaranteed employment, free housing, and low infant mortality rates. Luckily, some American lanyards (and a few billion dollars from oligarchs and Western interests) helped swing

---

ROMAN EMPIRE

117 AD

SIZE: From Britannia to Persia, Lusitania to Axum

LEADERS: Augustus Caesar, Marcus Aurelius, Trajan

MOTTO: *Senatus Populusque Romanus*

GREATEST ACHIEVEMENTS: Built roads, amphitheaters, and aqueducts that stand to this day; killed Christ

DOWNFALL: Vandalism

the election for Yeltsin. He repaid the good faith of his country's citizens (and the loans of his benefactors) with more privatization, eventually handing power to former KGB officer and competitive CrossFitter Vladimir Putin.

Putin proceeded to turn Russia into a supercharged version of America, with all the bigotry, inequality, and sham-democracy that went along with it. When Putin's new souped-up national-capitalist aggro-state sought to reclaim the sphere of influence it had lost after the fall of Communism, was the US proud of the precious, rapacious child it had raised? No! First, Mitt Romney identified Russia as America's biggest global threat in 2012, and then, four years later, all the liberals who had giggled at that bit of backward-looking hysteria decided that Mitt was right after all and that a good way to #resist President Cheeto would be to send antiaircraft missiles to the Babi Yar Reenactment Society in Ukraine. Some people and some countries just can't take yes for an answer.

ITALY

2018

SIZE: Boot

LEADERS: Bunga bunga master who owns a TV network, anyone in the "sanitation business"

MOTTO: When you're here, you're family

GREATEST ACHIEVEMENTS: "I am, ehhh, how you say, artista. Come to my appartamento, I show you my *cazzo*."

DOWNFALL: Mistress refused to have third abortion

Euro-America

With the former Soviet Union foreclosed on, the last real threat to American global hegemony had been eliminated.* The future looked bright enough to necessitate shades, so to speak. The final piece of the project was to create a single market out of the hodgepodge of fractious cheese-producing nations in Europe.

Once the danger of Soviet invasion was gone, the ruling classes could begin turning Europe into a slightly grimier version of EPCOT. All the continent's distinct nationalisms, with their meatballs and blackface Santas, would be preserved as local flair, while economic and political power were centralized in the headquarters of the new European Union. Unfortunately for the globalist

---

* Except for the emerging public-private partnership of China, but how much of a threat could they ever become?

AMERICAN EMPIRE

2018

PRESIDENT: Donald Trump

GREATEST CITIES: New York, Los Angeles, Orlando

OPPOSITION LEADERS: Chuck Schumer, Nancy Pelosi, Jimmy Kimmel

MOTTO: *E Pluribus Unum*

MILITARY: $639,000,000,000 budget, over one million under arms, bases in over 150 countries

DOWNFALL: Read the rest of the book, dummy

schemers, European national identity proved more resilient than anticipated—something Slobodan Milošević could have told them in between genocides. So instead of going forward with political unification (dead-on-arrival), they went through the back door with a currency-based union, figuring that with time, the political institutions would catch up with the reality on the ground.

But a funny thing happened on the way to the End of History: a financial crisis in 2008 that the Euro system was completely incapable of handling. You can't totally blame them; they were told that capitalism had won, and this kind of thing really wasn't supposed to happen anymore. Despite that, the European Central Bank responded to the '08 crisis with a Wahhabist-style neoliberal austerity that even the moderate consensus-makers in Washington didn't have the stomach for. Cue permanent immiseration in the peripheral states of the Euro (the so-called PAWGs) who couldn't devalue their currency to boost exports, and aid so-called labor reform in

---

N E 0 M E R I C @

2041

PROCONSUL: Logan Paul

GREATEST CITIES: SeaSteadia, the Walmart in Columbus, Ohio, that isn't completely flooded, New York (still the #1 greatest, classiest city in the world, baby. Go Yanks, Mets, Giants, Jets, Knicks, Nets, Rangers!!)

OPPOSITION LEADERS: The Morlock Conclave, Immortan Musk, the second coming of Jesus Christ

MOTTO: No Xans, No Lean, Smoke Purp

MILITARY: Three gigantic biomechanical beings known as "Evangelions," or "Evas" for short, piloted by three unique and gifted teenagers who possess nervous systems capable of melding with the cybernetic creatures

DOWNFALL: Shinji refuses to pilot his Eva

the rest of Europe. Today Europe can be divided into the countries with sun, good weather, great food, and sex but terrible economies and those with great economies but total darkness, awful food, and even worse sex. However, all of Europe remains strongly united against male circumcision, and as such is still far, far ahead of America.

All this economic hardship, coupled with a spiraling refugee crisis and the continued inability of political institutions to address any of it, has led to a big retro-trend across the continent: That's right, the thirties are back! Dance marathons! Art Deco! The rise of organized fascist political movements!

You WoT, Mate?

Let us put aside this corporate fable of the American Century and turn now to the world you know and love. At the time of this writing, the War on Terror is now in its seventeenth year, becoming, as NatSec intellectuals like to put it, "a generational commitment." It has gone from the unprecedented, epoch-defining focus of our national destiny to something we all just meekly accept and largely tune out as it hums along in the background as kids born in September 2001 reach military age. US policy currently involves allying with the "moderate" elements of Al Qaeda and the Taliban against newer, evil-er kinds of terrorists and their state sponsors. Outside of this very easy and base irony, one can assess the value of the war by entertaining a simple thought experiment: How much safer would both America and the rest of the world be right now if our government's response to 9/11 was to pretend it didn't happen and do absolutely nothing?

Would the Middle East be the cauldron of violence it is today? Would ISIS exist? Would we witness the same number of terrorist attacks in Europe? Would a million or so people have been killed in Iraq and Afghanistan? Almost certainly not. But remember, for the national security class and the small cadre of Ford administration has-beens who came to power before 9/11, all these details are features, not bugs, of the War on Terror. The cascade of atrocities and disasters that issued forth from this US-led crusade, from ISIS snuff films to sectarian bloodletting to institutionalized torture to mass surveillance to the refugee crisis to an American culture warped by militarism and troop worship, is just further justification for why we must stay the course. Your ability to safely work in an office building, go to a concert, run a marathon, take mass transit, or fly in an airplane free from any unplanned inconveniences is at best incidental, and at worst actively hostile, to the goals and logic of the War on Terror.

The thing we call the War on Terror is, like pretty much every other war, a crude land grab for control of resources, oil pipelines, and good old-fashioned access to markets. The national security state used the pretext of 9/11 and the blowback from the Cold War as ways to drum up a chintzy version of the war economy from World War II and replace our fucked-up retail-debt economy after we killed the golden goose of American industry and manufacturing.

Now, we don't want to give you the impression that it's all just simply blood for oil. A great deal of the blood is indeed being exchanged for oil, but the people who dreamed up this never-ending story think American control of the world's oil supply is but a perk compared to restoring America's martial spirit and imperial

Infobox: Terms for NatSec Wonks in Other Countries

The world lay in ruins in the aftermath of the Second World War. The Allied victors knew mankind could not survive another cataclysm. In order to skirt destruction on a biblical scale, postwar leaders would resort to an affront to God even more devastating than nuclear weapons: wonks.

When tensions between the Soviet Union and the United States flared in a divided Berlin immediately after the war, both powers and their respective allies began stockpiling as many wonks as they possibly could. These technocrats were given the task of advising presidents, prime ministers, or really anyone who had similar backgrounds to the wonks themselves.

Now they're a staple of modern government. Across all nations, wonks' identifiable traits are social ineptitude and physical disagreeableness. Their habitats are foundations and think tanks. The only way they differ is in how they're named. Below are samples of different wonk-nomenclature from across the globe.

RUSSIA: Mysl' truslivyy (Thought Coward)

CHINA: Cèsuǒ tàijiàn (Toilet Eunuch)

JAPAN: Hiretsuna akushū basutādo (Dishonorable Stench Bastard)

FRANCE: Crétin fétiche (Fetish Moron)

UNITED KINGDOM: Spreadsheet Cunt

POLAND: Francuz (Frenchman)

SWEDEN: Skogsidiot (Forest Imbecile)

SOUTH KOREA: Laeteuwa mun saiui geunchinsang-gan chulsaeng-ui geeuleun adeul (Lazy Son Born of Incest between Rat and Moon)

INDONESIA: Pantat basah (Wet Ass)

GERMANY: [banned]

ISRAEL: בתולה שימושית (Useful Virgin)

BRAZIL: Pé obsessivo (Foot Obsessive)

SPAIN: Error en el blog (Blog Failure)

DENMARK: Frosne kønsorganer (Frozen Genitals)

SAUDI ARABIA: Alyahudi (Jew)

NORTHERN VIRGINIA: Tier-One Operator

vigor. The fact is, we've been gun-shy about being a great power since Vietnam and pathetically idle since the end of the Cold War robbed us of a worthy adversary. The Twin Towers imploding on national television was just what we needed to put some fire in our bellies, spring in our steps, and vengeance in our hearts. For a Straussian, endless and aimless struggle against evil is just what the doctor ordered for our hyperindividualized and alienated culture, not to mention a great way to keep military budgets and their pleated trousers swole. The War on Terror is the bathtub our empire lies in, surveying a sunset over a wheat field in the Cialis commercial that is our twenty-first-century international statecraft.

While pretty much any president—including the one who actually won the 2000 election—would have attacked Afghanistan after 9/11, only George W. Bush and company were in the right place at the right time to really get this bigger project off the ground. In the words of Donald Rumsfeld: Afghanistan lacked any "good targets" to obliterate—and so it was off to Iraq. They wanted a twenty-first-century world stage dictated by American military might, and refused to accept a multipolar world in which powers simply used diplomacy to jockey for advantage. For the neocons and the defense establishment, though, that would be heresy, because we have the biggest military in the world, and, in the words of Madeleine Albright, "What's the point of having this superb military you're always talking about if we can't use it?" Sure, America can "negotiate" with other powers, but always "from a position of strength"—i.e., a big military presence where all the oil is.

Anyway. There's no point in litigating the Iraq War too much. It's the defining disaster of this new American Century. It should be sufficient to say that the justifications for it, from WMD to any supposed concern for the freedom and well-being of the Iraqi people, were obvious confabulations that fooled only those who wanted to be conned and those who just didn't care because the thought of war excited them so much. This included pretty much all the media, government, and cultural elites of this country, and it remains the gold standard for how we should judge them. (One demographic decidedly *not* fooled was black Americans, almost 70 percent of whom opposed the war out of some sense that America is actually kind of bad.*) Meanwhile, our thought leaders in the government and media stuck with it as bravely as they could through the rising body counts and the Abu Ghraib revelations until around 2007, when they were finally forced by Bush's top-to-bottom incompetence to give up the ghost.

By then, everyone reluctantly realized that there wasn't going to be any good ending or VJ Day moment that would retroactively make their support of the Iraq War look noble or wise. They realized the money and credibility they invested in this project—clinched by a particularly impressive Herbalife presentation at the UN—was simply not coming back.

However, this is America, and in our country, no dream ever really dies. In this case, we were able to swap out George W. Bush for General David Petraeus as 2007's figure of national leadership and competence and trade "Mission Accomplished" for "Uh, the Surge Worked?" And that was that. The Iraq War didn't

---

* Jeffrey M. Jones, "Blacks Showing Decided Opposition to War," *Gallup*, March 28, 2003, http://news.gallup.com/poll/8080/blacks-showing-decided-opposition-war.aspx.

demonstrate American might or benevolence on the global stage the way we might have hoped, nor did it inspire any new national purpose or credo. But it was no real loss, either, because not a single person involved was ever held accountable, save for Chelsea Manning.

And then, in 2008, we got Obama, the living refutation of swaggering idiot cowboys like Bush and snarling, sneering blood drinkers like Cheney. Nevertheless, Obama pulled off a much trickier job: Febreze-ing our national conscience without ever truly reckoning with what happened or winding down our blood-soaked "strategic interests in the region." Despite Obama's gloss as a liberal beacon of hope, this was the moment the War on Terror stopped being an emotional spectacle in American life and became a new baseline for reality. It joined the background static of our society, with the imprimatur of both parties and therefore all acceptable points of view. It became something that simply *is*, existing perfectly outside the realm of politics and ideology. The days of "boots on the ground" and "nation-building" were over, and the phrase "War on Terror" now meant harnessing our technology to manage a global drone assassination campaign. We could even safely retire "War on Terror," as the thing itself no longer required a name, so thoroughly metastasized was it throughout our body politic.

All this was far less upsetting for the public—the American public, that is—but all the more corrosive to our souls, precisely because of how invisible and consequence-free it now appears.

Still, it should be noted that while they may be out of power for now, the architects of the War on Terror remain at large. They're ensconced in the Virginia and Maryland suburbs, in think tanks, op-ed sections, and on cable news. Some have even taken up positions as leaders of the #Resistance to President Trump, but none of them have lost hope for a new Pax Americana. Their mission remains the same. For these "heroes in error," the real prize is still, and always was, Iran. The Islamic Republic. The Shia Succubus. Iraq is just a *Scrabble* tile away from Iran, and while Saddam's old stomping ground was merely supposed to be a launching pad toward the rest of the Middle East, Iran was always the real treasure, the site of a new, glorious, liberated American dominion to print AEI pamphlets and pump petro-dollars.

Iran is our real enemy because, for our national security planners, it represents the unthinkable: a genuine regional power with its own oil resources outside the US fold that isn't a complete basket case. As such, we're treated to the semiregular cant that Iran is the "greatest exporter of terrorism" in the world and—even more galling, considering who's saying it—that it's "meddling in the region" and is a "threat to its neighbors." This is also why it's considered gauche to bring up Saudi Arabia's state sponsorship of terrorism and Wahhabism. For American NatSec intellectuals, be they of the Brookings Institution or the American Enterprise Institute, killing three thousand Americans and engineering the worst famine of the twenty-first century in Yemen is *far* more forgivable than getting away with an Islamic Revolution for forty years. This is why Saudi Arabia remains in good standing in the media and think tank zone, despite being patient zero for Islamic fundamentalism and terror.

The End of the World Chapter As We Know It

Conservative pundits love to compare America to Rome, mainly because they want to be allowed to drape sheets around their asses and bring back slavery and man-boy love. But that doesn't mean it's not a useful analogy. Like Rome, we're a deluded and decadent empire in terminal decline.

After a brief postwar golden era (for white people), the end of the twentieth century saw America open up the world economy so much that we stopped making things at all and just started buying them elsewhere to support our British, German, and South Asian pals. Nowadays it's *other* people who make things—not least our erstwhile Communist enemy, China. Despite the gaudy, ongoing celebrations of American Exceptionalism, this country has been reduced to being the military arm of international capital: demoted from manager to rent-a-cop. Everything's on credit, with a precarious and doomed balance between military spending and domestic debt.

Meanwhile, China, carved up by Europe in the nineteenth century, expelled those powers in the twentieth. They kicked off this century with a supercharged, state-guided capitalism that's carrying out the most mind-boggling planned industrialization in world history.* They're developing domestic markets, not just exports, and

---

* From 1901 to 2000, America used 4.5 billion tons of cement. A couple years ago, China started buying a lot of cement. They went through 6.6 billion tons in just three years. Analysts fear that by the end of the decade, China will have more half-pipes per capita than the US.

starting up their own imperial designs in Africa—the last remaining spot on the planet yet to be turned into a base for cheap industrial manufacturing. In twenty years, that pang you get when you see "Made in China" on a clothing tag will be replaced by a wince from seeing "Made in Africa," and it may even sting a little more. But China is doing just what America's done—what the world's been doing—for the last two hundred–odd years: consuming and growing more and more each year, with no end in sight, driven by a deep, deep madness.

So brace yourself for a lot more talk about a showdown between democratic Western values and mammoth, red, Communist China, and remember that it's all total horseshit. It's just cover for a desperate scramble for resources on our wheezing, dying planet, as every country's elites pile up last bits of obscene wealth to better withstand the inevitable collapse.

And what a collapse it will be! As Thomas Friedman pointed out in his thought-provoking bestseller *Our Interconnected World*, the world is more interconnected than ever. Ideas, capital, racist memes, and state repression flow through borders at the speed of imagination. Thanks to the digital revolution, a neo-Nazi in Budapest can now obtain a list of local Roma and their addresses from an anime-obsessed hacker in Quezon City on a platform funded by a paleolibertarian transhumanist venture capitalist in San Jose who is at that instant explaining the plot of *Atlas Shrugged* to a yawning high-class cam girl in Johannesburg, all at the click of a button. For you and the transnational ruling class, this means that world capitalism is churning toward its brutal denouement at maximum efficiency.

Yes, the world's future is a veritable Choose Your Own Adventure of impending cataclysms. Runaway wealth inequality dramatically expands the underclass as nations race to the bottom to cut wages in a futile effort to slam the brakes on the inexorably falling rate of profit; throw in resource scarcity and overconsumption and we get rationing of basic human necessities among the global poor and outrage among the Western upper classes when the rare earth metals needed to manufacture their animatronic *Boss Baby*–themed merchandise have been exhausted. Or we could just have a good old-fashioned global economic depression once the cheap-credit house of cards falls over.

Of course, no roster of anticipatable apocalypses would be complete without the total ecological collapse caused by climate change. It turns out that two centuries of spewing industrial effluvium into the atmosphere to power the modern world wasn't without its consequences. At the dawn of the Industrial Revolution, the amount of carbon dioxide in the atmosphere was around 280 PPM. As of this writing, we're over 410 PPM and rising. The concentration limit needed to prevent irreversible ecological damage is, uh, way less than that.

To be fair, it may be all right, as fossil-fuel industry scientists point out that the earth's atmosphere had similar CO_2 concentrations during such periods as the Solar Death Epoch and the Uninhabitable Era (a misleading name, given the various genera of bedbug that prospered during this period). We aren't looking to cause a panic or anything, but to be perfectly honest, you should put this book down right now and look up the cost of a decommissioned missile silo in Svalbard.

We don't have to tell you what climate change has wrought. You see the headlines on the Weather Channel website when you're just trying to find out whether you need an umbrella today. It's a five- to seven-degree-Fahrenheit increase in the global mean temperature (and that's if we do nothing), ocean acidification (permanent end to Red Lobster's Crabfest), half a meter or so of sea-level rise (which has already inundated a few insular countries), destruction of millions of acres of arable land (increased property values in the Yukon Territory), food insecurity, water insecurity, the return of ancient comic-book-villain-origin-story-caliber diseases unearthed from melted permafrost, immensely destructive tropical storms that cause precipitous drops in approval ratings for Republican administrations, sharp reduction of biodiversity, albedo effect, feedback loop, polar ice caps melting, malaria, war, refugees, Lenny Bruce is not afraid.

People talk about the "coming apocalypse." Take a closer look. The apocalypse is Puerto Rico annihilated by a hurricane. It's villages in India, Bangladesh, and Nepal tortured by lethal flooding.

The apocalypse is already here; you just don't live there yet.

Not too long ago, scientists agreed that a global temperature increase of two degrees Celsius was the absolute upper limit for preventing environmental catastrophe. This was the starting point for global negotiations to reduce carbon emissions. The international community, fully cognizant of the consequences of their actions—as directed by the US and rising countries like China and India, who felt left out of the first Industrial Revolution—said "Eat my ass" and ignored the warnings. The cutthroat cost-benefit analysis they offered was that transitioning to clean, renewable sources of energy would slow down economic development to an unacceptable extent. China and India wanted to know why they couldn't litter their countryside with CO_2-spewing, coal-burning power plants when countries like America and Britain built their wealth (and colonial empires) in the past century doing the same. And developing countries in places like Africa and Central America that have never enjoyed the fruits of a stupid consumerist society like ours had a thing or two to say about their resources being pillaged and their environment being destroyed to ensure that middle-class Americans and Chinese can afford Chaturbate tokens.

If a bleeding-heart cuck socialist atheist liberal professor were to become president of the United States, even they wouldn't have the moral authority to say to people living in the *Slumdog Millionaire* reality, "You know what, we may have had our heyday stealing your resources and spewing noxious gases into the atmosphere to build a rich and entitled middle class, but you guys need to knock it off because the insurance premiums on our beachfront condos are getting out of control." (And that's *if* the American ruling class wanted to do something about climate change.)

Europe, populated as it is with self-loathing environment-loving sexual deviants, has tried to do its part, starting a continental cap-and-trade market that has accomplished little more than making bicyclists in Amsterdam feel smug and reducing the spot price of crude oil so developing countries can get cheaper dirty energy. Of course that's before the US pulled out of the already watered-down and woefully insufficient Paris Agreement altogether.

So peace out, globalists. You can take away my diesel-burning backyard smelter when you pry it from my cold, dead hands.

Nobody wants to deal with the hangover from two centuries of untrammeled environmental extermination. Every earnest attempt at even ameliorating the effects of climate change has failed dramatically, and each time someone tried, global capitalism snuck away with cookie crumbs on its face, pausing only to make a cutesy "Who, me?" face to the camera right as another Bangladeshi village got buried in mudslides.

Capitalism would be moribund even in the absence of all this; climate change just gives an exciting, breakneck, life-and-death impetus to this struggle coming down the pike. It's the Splash Mountain of teleologies. The dislocations created by climate change helpfully remind us that the political systems we live under are incapable of solving any fundamental problems or acting in the interests of anyone but the ruling class—and no number of bright-eyed Brookings Institution–trained technocrats can change that.

I Ain't Blogging Anymore

As business mindset futurist experts, we can tell you that these trends will lead to more nationalism, more terrorism, more weapons, more wars, more fracturing of the creaky global order in which the real enemies of humanity will never be identified so long as there's an inexhaustible supply of people who don't look like you to scapegoat, and more walls put up by rich countries to keep out those folks lining up just to get down.

And if the global order can't even get its act together to forestall an imminent threat to its own survival, what should make you think it could handle any number of looming self-inflicted technological crises? Take a moment to imagine what new and exciting crowd-control weapons Elon Musk will sell to your government in the next few years. Think about what every country now understands about the human genome and what biological weapons will exist by the end of the next decade. The United States already spends well over half a trillion dollars a year on its military to defend against . . . what? Obviously, a handful of nukes alone would be enough to ward off any attempt to violate our territorial integrity, but goddammit, we need more to maintain our imperial dominion over a shrinking segment of a dying world. The rest of the global populace is still, understandably, not happy about this state of affairs.

For how long is this situation tenable? You don't have to be the main character in the first third of a YA novel to realize we're going to end up in a very bad place.

We're sure that you, the idiot reader so stupid as to buy this book, can imagine a global order built on egalitarianism—one in which the productive forces of society aren't spent on inventing new weapons of mass destruction and clever ways to brutalize dissidents but on ensuring that all people enjoy the fruits of their birthright, an order that holds human beings and their fundamental rights as sacrosanct, that believes the provision of basic human needs to be the sole objective of politics and the economy, that rejects violence and militarism in toto.

But that's not your world. Sorry to bum you out. The rest of this book is kind of funny, though.

CHAPTER TWO

LIBS

What did liberals do that was so offensive to the Republican Party, Senator? I'll tell you what they did. Liberals got women the right to vote. Liberals got African Americans the right to vote. Liberals created Social Security and lifted millions of elderly people out of poverty. Liberals ended segregation. Liberals passed the Civil Rights Act, the Voting Rights Act. Liberals created Medicare. Liberals passed the Clean Air Act, the Clean Water Act. What did conservatives do? They opposed every one of those programs. Every one. So when you try to hurl the word liberal *at my feet as if it were something dirty, something to run away from, something that I should be ashamed of, it won't work, Senator, because I will pick up that label and wear it as a badge of honor.*

—**MATT SANTOS, *THE WEST WING***

If the rule you followed brought you to this, of what use was the rule?

—**ANTON CHIGURH, *NO COUNTRY FOR OLD MEN***

rick a liberal, do they not bleed? Of course—they'll bleed all over you like a Romanov's second cousin. Do they not, like us, prefer things be good, rather than bad? In some very general sense, yes. And, as the first epigraph above lays out, do they not have a record of popular legislation to their name? To be sure, and boy, do they love to bring it up.

Why, then, do we hate the lib?

The essential problem is not that liberals are "as bad" as conservatives but rather that there is a giant sucking void at the core of their being. In place of real beliefs, liberals have guilty consciences; in place of politics, they have a Democratic Process to assuage those consciences. This process pits tepid reforms against a deranged and revanchist right wing with no such inclination toward consensus or incrementalism. Despite its claim to the mantle of American Progress, the liberal algorithm produces positive social change or legislation only when pressured—sometimes terrorized—by militant and/or popular left-wing movements. Without an organized and popular Left, liberals end up negotiating themselves into oblivion, moving the country, inevitably, to the right.

If you're of the millennial generation and even slightly left of center, liberals and the Democratic Party have been the only game in town as long as you've been alive. Your parents most likely protested the Vietnam War and supported the civil rights movement, and have been patting themselves on the back ever since. But the litany of bold, progressive legislation liberals always point to is at *least* thirty years old, and it's been eroded by both Republican and Democratic governments since. All those great liberal achievements have been systematically dismantled both by the Right—who've made such destruction their mission—and Democrats and liberals themselves, who believe they have to "innovate" their ideas and move to the center to win elections.

(Yes, yes, we know that *liberal* and *Democrat* are not actual synonyms. But by the time of FDR, the party's central leadership was liberal. And with LBJ, it had generally become the liberal party, while the Republican Party shed all its John Lindsays and Ed Brookes and fully blossomed into a pulsating, Jesse Helms–shaped blob.)

Your parents likely considered themselves pretty radical when they were your age. They were known to enjoy "good vibrations," solid wages backed by union power, a college education that cost a nickel, and the ability to go to the doctor without selling their car to pay for it. But since those days, America has jerked to the right, and so liberals had to do the same in order to win elections and keep the country from moving further right!

This is the basic liberal mantra, and it's fitting that it takes the form of an excuse. Its end result is a political system irrevocably weighted toward the forces of reaction. Coincidentally, by almost every metric, you are poorer and your life is more precarious than your parents' were at a similar age. Get over it, snowflake; this book is your participation trophy.

Unfortunately, the eternal wimp-out shows no signs of slowing down. These days, there are two kinds of liberals: those who vote for Democrats because the alternative is worse, and those who get teary-eyed at the thought of supporting Cory Booker or some similarly phony slug. The latter are just moderate Republicans and should be written off completely. The former deserve better but probably have some misplaced attachment to the political tradition of "standing up" to the right wing. These poor souls can be spared the Chapo Reeducation Center (with our patented Lib-ovico Treatment), but only if they have imbibed the lessons and history laid out in this chapter and inform on their parents to the Chapo Central Committee.

We're Only *Kind* of Evil: Libs throughout American History

Much of the American history you learned in your ACLU-funded madrassa would have you believe that America was founded by a mix of religious zealots, genocidal frontiersmen, and slave owners. That history is correct. However, it ignores the fact that for every ten rugged, conservative types you read about, there was at least one dainty tattletale willing to make a stand for peace, justice, and *compromise.* We don't know much about these men and women because they utterly failed to achieve either peace or justice in the blood-dimmed tide of American history.

But this tradition lives on today—for example, in the words of Uncle Joe Biden, who in fall 2017 laid down this wisdom: "Even in the days when I got there, the Democratic Party still had seven or eight old-fashioned Democratic segregationists. You'd get up and you'd argue like the devil with them. Then you'd go down and have lunch or dinner together. The political system worked. We were divided on issues, but the political system worked."

People like Biden have been present all through history. Despite not always having a word for their beliefs, these brave souls were early ancestors of the modern American liberal. Let us now take a brief trip through time and shed light on some history even Howard "Big Dick" Zinn probably didn't tell you about.

Bell, Cory Booker, and Candle

In colonial New England, most people's lives were defined by hard work, NoFap, and an austere Puritanical religion that offered scant opportunity for undoing the belt on your hat and having a good time. Perhaps the only moment a good Pilgrim could get a bit loose was during one of the periodic outbreaks of mass hysteria that would crop up whenever a dairy cow's milk went sour, a goat looked weird, or a widow stood to inherit any amount of property. Agents of the devil were afoot. In the sweep of witch fever across seventeenth-century Massachusetts, one can see the stirrings of an early form of American liberalism: those who sought to reform the badly outdated witch-identifying standards and practices of their communities. Towns like Salem, Ipswich, and others were unfortunately stuck in Calvinism 1.0, badly in need of better data on women seeking congress with the devil.

Social reformers emerged from these dark, narrow New England glens to champion "reality-based" witch trials: Men like Abstinence True-Facts and Josias Goodmen-Project pushed back against the pervasive ignorance and prejudice of their time, fighting for higher standards of evidence, as well as more humane punishments for those convicted of consorting with the dark side, such as the right to be burned at the stake by a mob of your peers. They engaged in spirited and respectful debate with the social conservatives of their day, men like Joseph Glanvill and Cotton Mather. Indeed, True-Facts and Goodmen-Project defended famous witch trial defendant Sarah Good on the grounds that the spectral evidence introduced against her was procured illegitimately. They issued scathing takedowns of Cotton Mather's *Wonders of the Invisible World* for being improperly footnoted.

Unfortunately, Good was executed anyway, and for their brave stand for the rule of law, science, and human rights, both men were prosecuted and covered with stones until their bodies were crushed. It's rumored that Goodmen-Project's last words to the Court of Oyer and Terminer were, "Thou art not aware of how most foule thou appeareth at this moment."

For these early American libs, being crushed to death by stones was a small price to pay for being on the right side of history. By insisting that more than one eyewitness was needed to confirm a sighting of an apparition, these bleeding-heart Puritans helped save the lives of countless women who would have otherwise been lost to shoddy or, at times, completely unfounded accusations of getting head from Beelzebub.

Our Revolution

In the lead-up to the American Revolution, relations between the thirteen colonies and Britain were strained by the issue of the Crown's aggressive taxation. With the passage of the Stamp Act, enraged patriot groups, such as the Sons of Anarchy, took up "No taxation without representation" as a rallying cry. At the same time, lesser-known nationalist groups like the Project for an Independent America (PIA) also organized around the issue of taxation, but unlike the scruffier roving patriot gangs, the PIA actually wanted *more* taxation to pay for charter apprenticeships and programs to teach children to tie complicated sailor's knots, the eighteenth-century equivalent of coding.

Emphasis on "Civil" War

The greatest liberal icon of the first half of the nineteenth century was undoubtedly Henry Clay, fittingly known as the "Great

Compromiser" for his preternatural ability to bring both sides together. Clay understood that at the end of the day, everyone—Whig or Democrat, slave owner or abolitionist, Irishman or human—was a white male landowner and ought to put their differences aside and come together over a cup of switchel to hash out pragmatic policies that would work for every member of the ruling class. To that end, Clay designed the Compromise of 1850, a package of reforms he helped pass by telling Southerners, "If you like your slaves, you can keep them." Clay's Compromise stands as a towering achievement for radical moderation and centrism that managed to postpone a bloody Civil War for just under decade.

During the prelude to the Civil War, proto-liberals began to solidify their identity and soundly supported the cause of abolition. However, they were still wary of opposing the evil institution *too* vociferously, lest they become the very thing they hated. Ever vigilant for ways to demonstrate their moral superiority, Civil War libs sent around a collection plate to raise funds for the damage done to Harpers Ferry by the radical extremist John Brown, preaching, "This is *not* who we are." In a last-ditch effort to bring the Southern states back into the Union, libs put forth the Crittenden Compromise, a bold piece of bipartisan legislation mandating that the Constitution could never be amended to end slavery, and in exchange slaves would receive tariff credits they could use to buy their freedom after sixty years of labor.

After the war, Southern whites protested Reconstruction by

requesting taverns and general stores take their orders for corn pone and gingham skirts under the names "General Lee" and "Nathan Bedford." Reconstruction-era libs responded by buying more cornpone and gingham. The Compromise of 1877 was another landmark of civil moderation: on the one hand, it prevented Democrat Samuel J. Tilden from winning the presidency, and on the other hand, the antebellum slave-owning aristocracy regained total political control of the South, engaged in violent repression of freedmen, reinstalled the institution of slavery in all but name, and perpetuated a racial crisis that would last for the next 141 years and counting—so, win-win. One can picture the ancestors of today's libs standing by, hands over hearts.

Spread the Gild Around

The rapid consolidation of capital that followed the Civil War put American industrialization into overdrive, spraying mechanized jets of diarrhea into the faces of average Americans. For some reason, very few people—be they former yeoman farmers driven from their land by collapsing commodity prices or immigrants seeking new lives in the New World—were thrilled with the deal offered by the rising robber-baron class: short, miserable lives spent toiling in mills, factories, and mines in exchange for twice-weekly ice deliveries to their hovels. Riots and strikes exploded in the last decades of the nineteenth century as laborers sought to reduce the danger and drudgery of their work and increase their wages, or at least to jack those ice deliveries up to three times a week.

Liberals of a rising middle class responded by forming the

Progressive movement, which ushered in the uncreatively named Progressive Era.

The Progressives sought to soothe the anger and militancy of the restive working class by placing government restrictions on industry. Sure, they took up the demands for eight-hour workdays, safety regulations, and the end of child labor that workers had been making for years and brought them to the seat of power. But they added their own uniquely liberal policy prescriptions as well. After all, what good would it be to lighten the workload of common laborers if their culture of victimhood and laziness persisted? In order to take advantage of the many exciting new job tracks in the fast-changing industrial economy (powder monkey, gear gibbon, axle ape, coal eater), workers would have to cultivate the bourgeois values of thrift and diligence.

Thankfully, Progressives conceived of a smart policy that would nudge the teeming urban hordes into lives of rewarding employment: eugenics. By pairing up the most intelligent and physically robust of the laboring classes and using nimble public-private partnerships to permanently dissuade the less competitive from procreating, desirable cultural traits and skull shapes would be passed along to future generations as less-desirable ones perished. It was a win for taxpayers, who wouldn't have to foot the bill for jugs of liquor and frayed overalls; a win for employers, who could count on a ready supply of well-bred workers; and especially a win for the congenitally undesirable workers themselves, who could bust nuts without fear of consequence.

The policy received a seal of approval from the US Supreme Court in 1927 when liberal lion Oliver Wendell Holmes Jr. ruled in

Buck v. Bell that state eugenics programs were constitutionally permissible. Holmes famously said, "Three generations of morons is enough," in his decision, a statement that would go on to be the slogan for ABC's TGIF lineup in the 1990s. The ruling coincidentally came just a month before Justice Holmes announced the opening of his own chain of "Uncle Ollie's Snip 'n' Clip" mandatory vasectomy clinics.

Hey La! Hey La! We Stand Tall: FDR

The administration of Franklin Delano Roosevelt began at the height of a major crisis of capitalism. During his historic inauguration speech, FDR famously declared "Fear ain't for me" and that he wasn't "into that foo-foo lame shit." The Roosevelt years smashed the record for consecutive presidential administrations and drove the pace car for twentieth-century American liberalism.

At a time when democracy was looking a bit worn-out compared to hot new trends like fascism and Communism, FDR's "Art of the Deal" set up a new, centralized state to not only manage the excesses of capitalism but also to project American power across the globe. It was an ambitious undertaking that sought to stave off a more radical politics creeping into society from the left: the president and his minions saw Communists unionizing black sharecroppers in the South and organizing sit-down strikes in the heart of Fordism and nervously proposed, "Hey, how about some, uh, public works projects and murals showing superjacked workers popping their biceps?"

The good things that came out of the New Deal: unions,

regulation of capital, massive investment in infrastructure, Social Security, seizing people's dumbass gold, dams, street art, and two-for-one happy hours. The bad thing: black people were excluded from pretty much all of it. FDR's administration systematically upheld white supremacy and segregation as a way to get the votes it needed from Southern Democratic politicians. (Also bad: Hello Mudda, Hello Fadda, Japanese Americans were sent to Camp Grenada, during World War II.)

And so, New Deal reforms ameliorated the worst of the Great Depression, but it took the completely top-down, centrally planned economy necessitated by waging total war against the Axis powers to fully end the Depression.

Postwar Consensus: Winter Warz

The Kennedys' Camelot is considered by many libs to be the high-water mark of postwar American liberalism. It's the administration every subsequent Democratic presidency is consciously and unconsciously compared to: a matinee-idol president with charisma, a pinch of exotic ethnicity (in 1960, many Americans still thought Catholics were a type of bipedal goat), and a cabinet full of Ivy League smarty-pantses. These were the people who would drag Eisenhower's stodgy, mothballed America across the New Frontier.

The Kennedy regime was in fact so bold and so beautiful that they bungled and equivocated on civil rights, steered America directly into the future bloodbath of Vietnam, and, during the Cuban Missile Crisis, stood ready to nuke the earth to a crisp if one Russian submarine commander hadn't slept in that morning.

For all liberalism's bragging about "getting things done," the only person who really got anything done during the Kennedy years was a young Marxist go-getter named Lee Harvey Oswald.

With that distraction out of the way, the rest of the sixties blew up all the contradictions of capitalism just as our country was finally gearing up to become a gay, latte-sipping social democracy. This was a time when America, fat and rich after World War II, took on huge deficits and propped up European and Japanese markets to lock down a global order of liberal capitalism. America was spraying gasoline everywhere, shouting, "My money's real good."

At the height of its power, America got a leader with a massive hog to match our massive empire: his name was Lyndon Baines Johnson, and he called his penis "Jumbo." *

Society Is Already Great

Despite being an egomaniacal, racist, Foghorn Leghorn man from Texas, Johnson was also a onetime schoolteacher who cared deeply about solving poverty. Through his dialectical synthesis of both tough guy *and* carelord, LBJ was shaping up to be the most powerful liberal politician who ever lived, eclipsing even Roosevelt (who was a bro, after all). Swept into office after a national tragedy, Johnson used his first inaugural address to call for a bold progressive agenda—not just a *good* society, mind you, but a *Great* Society. In an epic stem-winder brimming with biblical allusions and rich

* Robert A. Caro, *Master of the Senate: The Years of Lyndon Johnson* (New York: Vintage Books, 2003), 121.

barnyard analogies, Johnson rallied his Congress and his country behind civil rights, a war on poverty, health care reform, robust public education, and the inalienable right of every human being, regardless of race, color, or creed, to say the n-word.

But the contradictions of liberalism forced Johnson to trip over his mighty wang just as things were getting started, in a turn that would cannibalize the Democratic Party and end America's long liberal epoch: namely, the gory vortex of Vietnam. Technically, it was Eisenhower who initiated our presence there, but JFK deepened it, and LBJ positively juiced it. It wasn't conservatives who gave us full-blown slaughter in Vietnam—it was a cabinet of educated, elite, enlightened white liberals. And despite all the obvious signs of doomsday, the lamentations from the Left, and the daily horror show on the ground, they got their war. They dumped Agent Orange on farmers defending their land; they ran genocidal search-and-destroy missions, of which My Lai was merely the most famous example; they propped up a series of corrupt military dictatorships; they took a shit on the 1956 Geneva agreement that would have unified the country peacefully; their soldiers raped; their officers tortured; and they dropped more bombs on Vietnam than they did on the entirety of Europe and Japan during World War II. This, as ever, was the liberal compromise position, as most of the American Right wanted to use nukes. In any case, we effectively wiped a whole country off the map.

The liberal brain trust of America had carried out an

Indochinese holocaust—but for most libs, crazy as it sounds, Vietnam wasn't some horrible, pointless, bloody deviation. The sections of LBJ's speeches about alleviating poverty and creating a more just, egalitarian society at home *weren't contradicted* by the sections about "honoring our commitments" abroad (i.e., murdering people in Asia). They were part of the same mission. To this day, liberals view things like no-fly zones in Syria or microloans in Africa as extensions of their oh-so-enlightened social project at home. You see this kind of thought process when people react to the latest US mass shooting by saying something to the effect of, "These guns don't belong in American streets, they belong in their proper place: in the faces of Afghans and Iraqis."

Public disgust over Vietnam shot up year after year, but even that might not have been such a problem for Johnson if it weren't for the disintegration of America's supposed "consensus" on race. Riots in Watts, Newark, and Harlem exploded in the mid-sixties as black people struck back at round-the-clock police brutality, discrimination, and impoverishment. This was not a good turn of events for the touchy-feely Johnson administration's plan to "unite" and improve the country.

You don't need to study history to see how America reacts to uprisings of nonwhites on TV; you remember it from Ferguson in 2014 and Baltimore in 2015. The same things happened in the Johnson era: respectable liberals tut-tutted, responsible conservatives blamed the victims, and CHUDs bayed for race war. And, as with Ferguson and Baltimore, the Democrats in charge during the riots of the 1960s responded with vague bromides and tepid reforms rather than radical plans to end the deep-rooted racist systems that produced the unrest. (They also had the FBI mail every radical black leader a letter saying they were gay and should kill themselves—one of the last examples of liberals knowing how to troll people.) Meanwhile, the right wing, from John Birchers to Nixon's mafia—branded weirdos and squares only a couple of years before—tapped into the well of hopelessness, chaos, and white rage and prepared a tough-on-crime pitch to win back the country.

Liberalism was on the ropes. But instead of handling the challenges to his Great Society, LBJ stomped his feet, yelled, "I say, I say, I do believe I have the *vapors,*" and shipped thousands more Americans off to Vietnam.

Here's the potted history that usually follows: as the Right consolidated power, Vietnam cracked the Democratic Party, pitting pro-war union grunts against Black Panthers and college-educated hippies, which allowed the Republicans to co-opt the working class, a mass of lizard-brained lumpenproles. For the Right, this narrative proves conservatism was always the real answer for the American worker. For some socialists, it proves that well-intentioned 1960s radicals fucked up by alienating union power, the last bit of muscle on the left. And for liberals, it's completely obscured by their vivid memories of going to see psychedelic bands like Captain Freakout and thc Stillwater Jamboree. In every case, this story is another Cold War myth.

It's true that cigar-chomping union kingmakers like George Meany, head of the AFL-CIO, were a bunch of pro-war mummies. And it's true that Team Nixon exploited working-class resentment of rich-kid protesters amid "hard hat" rallies supporting the massacres in Vietnam. But the whole idea that the working class was uniformly pro-war and middle-class hippies were all against it is bullshit: polls and surveys at the time showed that proles were more antiwar than smug, college-educated elites.* This was the birth of a fake debate still raging today, with upper- and middle-class liberals slamming the dumb slugs of the working class as stupid, racist rubes—which is true to a point, but also covers up the enormous complicity of America's bourgeoisie in supporting awful wars, draconian conservative economics, and reactionary presidents like Nixon and Trump.

You can't just blame the baying hordes of plumbers and construction workers for Vietnam or the end of liberalism or the rise of Nixon. You certainly can't blame the counterculture or people of color. You can't even solely blame individual politicians like Johnson. So who can we blame, and why?

Truth is, the downfall of the liberal era was contained in its original triumph, the New Deal. That was a massive reshaping of government in response to outcry from the masses, a groundswell of popular rage over the failures of capitalism. But it was still

---

* Jefferson Cowie, *Stayin' Alive: The 1970s and the Last Days of the Working Class* (New York: New Press, 2010), 135, and Joshua B. Freeman, *Working-Class New York: Life and Labor Since World War II* (New York: New Press, 2001), 242.

a compromise, one meant to alleviate the pain of the Depression while retaining the basic structure of capitalism—its racial caste system included. Lyndon Johnson inherited that arrangement. The problem was, the compromise wasn't tenable. It demanded we use "growth" and redistribution to alleviate the contradictions of capital instead of radically changing (that is, equalizing) race and class relations altogether.

The liberal plan was to manage capitalism in a way that would reduce material injustice or want *just* enough to drain everyone's energy to build an alternative. And those alternatives were growing. On the race front, you had not only general unrest among black people and other minorities but also bona fide Marxist organizations like the Black Panthers. However well-meaning, Head Start and civil rights legislation weren't enough; African Americans were trapped in economically deprived areas, and there was no real plan to change that, since it would mean uprooting the hardwired racial caste system that FDR made and LBJ—for all his desire to *legally* improve the social order—was not interested in changing.

So, liberalism from FDR to Johnson was about accommodating white racism in its most quotidian form while eventually trying to tamp down its more old-fashioned form—i.e., *de jure* segregation and Jim Crow. But they did nothing to treat the disease, nothing radical that would have been necessary to actually solve the problem, which would have looked something like reparations and the wholesale rebuilding of urban neighborhoods. When that untenable situation devolved into riots, white flight—and therefore money flight—exacerbated the problem.

But it didn't stop there: since liberal capitalism was an imperial project, you had to enact this futile balance everywhere else as well. You had to be anti-Communist, with a whole anti-Communist foreign policy. So in the sixties, the generals and the wonks faced not only the Soviet menace but also third-world Marxists that needed to be put down. This necessitated destroying socialism as an alternative while also maintaining the military Keynesianism we utilized to get out of the Depression. After World War II, even though the size of the Army was reduced, its function as a subsidized industrial economy continued throughout the Cold War. And the thing is, when you spend years building all those weapons, eventually you gotta use 'em. And that South Asian people's movement is starting to look pretty dang uppity . . .

Carter: "Feeling Cute and Sad RN"

And so ended Big Dick Lyndon's reign, giving way to the equally maniacal, paranoid politics of Richard Nixon. Nixon's downfall came when enterprising journalists Bob Woodward and Carl Bernstein sexted with FBI agent Mark Felt to uncover the president's high crimes and misdemeanors. Incidentally, the authentic journalism of Woodward and Bernstein unleashed a brain bug into the skulls of American liberals, convincing them that all journalists were brave heroes and that one merely had to ask those in power, "Sir, how dare you, sir?" until they stepped down.

It worked on Nixon, after all. He did step down, and we ended up with Jimmy Carter, a man who did sweaters and offbeat farming long before horny Instagram poetry guys.

For some reason, Carter is remembered as wildly left-wing,

immortalized by conservatives as Satan incarnate and by liberals as proof that governing to your left is a losing ticket. They're right, too: Carter's pie-in-the-sky Marxist policies of deregulating trucking, airlines, and the credit industry while sending arms and cash to the proto-Taliban alongside Saudi Arabia and Pakistan's ISI—this stuff was just too idealistic. And so President Peanut-Lookin'-Ass-Boy lost to Ronald "I Smell Toast" Reagan in a triumph against ableism, causing liberals to hurl themselves back into the darkness until another weird centrist governor emerged from the South a decade later.

It's worth noting in the annals of Democratic/liberal feckless-ness that, in the 1980s, they *did* keep bona fide lunatic Robert Bork off the Supreme Court, which was a win. Still, despite controlling both houses of Congress during the second Reagan administration, they let a brain-dead right-wing president get away with carrying out an HBO miniseries's worth of Iran-Contra crimes, which was pathetic.

And here's a dose of irony to sweeten the pill: Reagan selling arms to Iran in order to fund rape squads in Central America really *did* make Watergate look like a "third-rate burglary." So if libs want to keep holding up Watergate as a historic triumph for the forces of good, they'll have to admit that letting Reagan off the hook represents a *far greater* historic triumph for the forces of evil. At least Nixon approved the EPA while he was blowing up the world; Reagan's run was an unabashed looting of the public sector. But at the time, in lib minds, the country simply couldn't go through another Watergate that would further erode Americans' respect for the institution of the presidency.

After all, it would still be a few more years until a leader would come along and jizz all over the Oval Office.

Premature Triangulation

If fake friend Jimmy Carter cleared the path for Reagan's assault on workers, poor people, and minorities, Bill Clinton picked up Ronnie's gun and put the dying New Deal out of its misery.

Clinton ran for president as a cerebral, charismatic figure who harnessed Boomer coolness to play the sax while sticking to the playbook of the right-leaning Democratic Leadership Council. This was a new club of losers who pushed an ideology frozen in time from the moment Reagan beat Walter Mondale, blaming every subsequent Democrat's loss on the party being too left-wing, too beholden to the Big Labor tax-and-spend policies that voters had supposedly rejected. Conceding most issues to the Right, Clinton perfected the "Third Way" politics that splits the difference between what the people you represent want and what the people who despise you want. (His counterpart in the UK, Tony Blair, carried out a similar revolution inside the Labour Party and, unsurprisingly, went on to chip away at the NHS and team up with George W. Bush on the Iraq War.)

This right turn would be one thing as a campaign strategy, but Clinton, the new and improved liberal, took this shit to heart. Once in office, he declared the era of big government over, "reformed" welfare by kicking a bunch of poor mothers off the dole, ballooned the prison population, vastly expanded the war on drugs, smashed a handful of small countries with bombs lest anyone call him a pussy, and made sure any gay people at the tip of the imperial spear could get killed but not married. The telecom act he signed into law is also the reason why you fucking hate your Internet service provider. Oh, and he demolished the firewall between commercial and investment banking, which set the stage for the greatest financial crash since that big Depression liberals are supposedly so proud of FDR for fixing.

For all his noble triangulating and compromising, Clinton was rewarded with a once-in-a-generation loss of Congress and his own impeachment and prosecution by a half dozen men actively receiving under-the-desk blow jobs from their mistresses during the Senate trial itself.

All the while, Clinton pushed liberals' dedication to compromise to the breaking point, testing their basic values by forcing them to back a man of obvious moral turpitude. Believe women? Not Juanita Broaddrick, Gennifer Flowers, or Paula "Drag a hundred dollars through a trailer park and there's no telling what you'll find" * Jones. Respect the Process? Not before you shunt your wife to a state she's never lived in to become senator because there just wasn't anyone else in the fourth-most-populous state who was better qualified for the job. Opposing, uh, eugenics? Clinton's welfare reform bill paid a $20 million prize to states willing to cut down on out-of-wedlock births. Opposing, uhhhhhh, slavery? In the Arkansas governor's mansion, Bill and Hillary enjoyed the services of unpaid black prisoners, a situation detailed in a passage of a book

---

* James Carville, quoted in Mike Royko, "Ok, So 'Trailer Trash' and 'Democrat' Not Always the Same," *South Florida SunSentinel*, January 29, 1997.

by Hilldawg that Bernie Sanders's oppo team should be liquidated for not having circulated:

> When we moved in, I was told that using prison labor at the governor's mansion was a long-standing tradition, which kept down costs, and I was assured the inmates were carefully screened. . . . I saw and learned a lot as I got to know them better. We enforced rules strictly and sent back to prison any inmate who broke a rule.*

Why did liberals stand by their man? After they'd spent twelve years out of the White House, was their despair so profound that they clung to a guy who kinda, sorta won two presidential elections? Were they simply so afraid of the resurgent Right that they felt they needed to triangulate just to stay relevant? Did he just remind them of John F. Kennedy because he was young and fucked around on his wife? Did they *agree with what he did*?

Beats us. Probably some combination of all of the above. But for as smart and as Process-respecting as liberals think Clintonism was, in practice it was a cascading series of desperate improvisations that diluted any ideological potency the Democratic Party had left. Executing a mentally disabled black man doesn't placate the Right?† Let's sign their flatly racist, eugenic welfare bill into law. That doesn't work? Let's legitimize their dehumanizing rhetoric and flatter their tribal instincts by calling young black men

---

* Hillary Clinton, *It Takes a Village* (New York: Simon & Schuster, 1996), 51–55.

† Peter Applebome, "Death Penalty; Arkansas Execution Raises Questions on Governor's Politics," *New York Times*, January 25, 1992.

"superpredators" and signing an anti–gay marriage bill into law. No dice? How about deregulating Wall Street banks—that ought to make suburban moderates like us, right? Oh fuck, why are we losing so many working-class voters???

Into the Wilderness: The Shrub Years

Despite harassment from the vaguely left-wing Bradley Buds, Clinton's VP, Al Gore, won the Democratic nomination in 2000. Gore attempted to chart a course between Clintonian triangulation and Naderite progressivism, inveighing against "Big Tobacco, Big Oil, the big polluters, the pharmaceutical companies, the HMOs" while promising to pragmatically maintain the economic prosperity of the 1990s. He chose as his running mate hawkish center-right senator Joe Lieberman (who would later become an independent and endorse John McCain in 2008). And as a sop to social conservatives, Gore dry-humped his wife onstage at the DNC to prove he was horny only for Tipper (who would later separate from Al in 2010).

Gore, of course, went on to shit the bed against an indigo child from Texas. His populist notes sounded insincere, coming as they did from the second banana of the DC establishment who famously went on *Larry King Live* to defend NAFTA. He hemorrhaged a few million lefty votes to Ralph Nader and, tied to his boss's policies while lacking his boss's charisma, lost eleven of the states Bill won in 1996.

But throughout it all, Gore respected the Process. While Bush traveled the country dissembling without a care, Gore prostrated himself before the judgment of Maureen Dowd and the *New York Times* op-ed page. When one of his advisors received a package containing Bush's debate prep materials, the advisor recused himself in the interest of fairness and reported the event to the FBI. (Super-fun fact: In 1980, Reagan was leaked papers from Carter's debate prep. He, of course, did the right thing and used them, because he wasn't nearly as much of a fucking sucker as institutional liberals.) In overtime, the GOP organized street mobs of Young Republican sociopaths—who would all later be rewarded with cushy jobs—to shut down the Florida recount while Lieberman went on TV to say late-postmarked absentee ballots (which favored Bush) should definitely be counted. The Bush campaign succeeded in sowing enough chaos and confusion that the Supreme Court stepped in to shut down the statewide recount, citing the legal doctrine of "Whatever."

Gore lost Florida—and thus the presidency—by 537 votes.

Bush's first term, quite frankly, broke liberals' brains. Deeply fearful of being smeared as unpatriotic, prominent liberal commentators, politicians, and publications fell over themselves to back the White House's Iraq War and wholesale evisceration of civil liberties. Funnily enough, this compromise didn't work. Senator Max Cleland, a triple-amputee Vietnam vet, was rewarded for his pro–Iraq War vote by getting called an Al Qaeda lover and losing his next election. Spooked by unexpected midterm losses in 2002, every establishment Democratic candidate for the presidency in 2004 also endorsed toppling Saddam. Howard Dean, a centrist triangulator from Vermont who likened himself to a moderate Republican in his own campaign book, emerged as the radical leftist candidate, because that's how awful things were.

It took a "quagmire" in Iraq, the failure of Bush's second-term agenda, the Old Testament–caliber destruction of a major American city, and a congressman sending horny instant messages to underage pages for the Dems to just *barely* retake Congress in 2006. But ask around and you won't hear the Democrats' midterm victory credited to the public's natural desire for change from a ruling party that had fucked up so immensely and been so thoroughly discredited.

You might hear it was because of foulmouthed (read: asshole) campaign chair Rahm Emanuel's strategy of pushing out weaker (read: leftier) candidates in favor of moderate (read: not gay) veterans and sheriffs to fight the perception that Democrats were weak on national security (read: not warmongers). Or you might hear it was because of the Democrats' "New Direction for America," a six-point platform featuring such revolutionary proposals as a tax deduction for college tuition.* You might even hear it was because of the goddamned Netroots.

In any event, liberals were ascendant. A card-carrying latte-swiller from San Francisco held the speaker's gavel, and if President Shrub wanted money for his war in Iraq or his trillion-dollar Wall Street bailout, by gum, he would have to ask nicely before receiving absolutely everything he requested. In the next cycle, Dems won historic supermajorities in both houses of Congress and, oh yeah, elected a black guy president.

---

* Chris Weigant, "A New Direction for America?" *Huffington Post*, June 23, 2006, https://www.huffingtonpost.com/chris-weigant/a-new-direction-for-ameri_b_23684.html.

Obungler's Omerica

Despite (or perhaps because of) his hilarious choice of running mate, John McCain was actually leading the polls until global capitalism totally collapsed, at which point voters decided to pick the constitutional law professor who talked real good instead of the drooling sundowner constantly babbling about bombing Iran.

Barack Hussein Ahmadinejad bin Laden Obama came into office with a 68 percent to 12 percent approval rating, the biggest Democratic House majority since the early nineties, and, by the middle of 2009, a filibuster-proof Senate majority. Since the financial crisis began, the Dow Jones had shed half its value, unemployment had climbed to a staggering 10 percent and rising, and the global economy had entered a profound recession. Millions of young activists—part of a generation loaded with debt and facing an unforgiving job market—stood ready to take marching orders from the man they helped put in the White House. Republicans were on the back foot, and society was primed for Obama to launch a generational transformation on par with the New Deal.

The young and ready president threw off his jacket, rolled up his sleeves, and declared, "Let's find some fucking consensus!"

Instead of Progressives, he packed his cabinet with retrograde Clintonites like Emanuel, Tim Geithner, Larry Summers, and, for some fucking reason, Hillary. Instead of a massive jobs program like the Civilian Conservation Corps, he passed a "stimulus" bill that included a greater number of dumbass tax cuts for businesses and mandatory social safety-net expenditures than countercyclical spending measures (about one-seventh of the bill contained actual infrastructure spending). Instead of nationalizing failed banks and frog-marching crooked Wall Streeters down lower Manhattan (like a young go-getter prosecutor named Rudy Giuliani did in the 1980s), Obama administered bailouts and begged creditors to start lending again. Instead of strengthening the right to organize unions like the National Industrial Recovery and Wagner Acts did, he refused to make card check—a system by which employees are allowed to unionize if they collect enough *Yu-Gi-Oh!* cards—a priority. Instead of cultivating his massive base of grassroots Obama for America volunteers to form a genuine movement, he folded them into the DNC out of the fear that—horror of horrors!—they might criticize him from the left. Instead of ensuring durable Democratic majorities by making Election Day a federal holiday, dismantling *Citizens United*, and admitting DC and Puerto Rico as states, he and the Democrats in charge of Congress refused to tamper with the filibuster (Process!). Obama himself only endorsed DC statehood well after his congressional majority had been squandered.

Instead of the transformation that was promised, we got the internalization of every wretched cop-out liberals had had beaten into them over the preceding four decades. Afraid of being called nanny staters? Hire libertarian dipshit Cass Sunstein to "nudge" workers into saving for retirement. Afraid of being called partisan? Water down your own legislation in a vain attempt at compromise, then watch it get passed on party lines anyway. Afraid of being called socialist? Pass an inscrutable market-based health care bill cribbed from the Heritage Foundation. Afraid of being called a spendthrift? Put an arbitrary limit on the stimulus bill that's supposed to *save the fucking economy*. Afraid of being called weak?

Compile an extrajudicial kill list and order your fleet of murderbots to bump off an American citizen and his son.

A funny thing happened on the way to throwing Chelsea Manning into horrendous solitary confinement: despite his deliberate, Rahm-managed gestures intended to show voters that he's a rational moderate (such as killing Osama bin Laden, the guy literally everyone agreed was bad), Obama was nevertheless attacked as a dog-eating, pork-barrel-spending, troop-murdering, Moon God–worshipping Communist. His cautious approach to governance and respect for the Process were rewarded with a historic loss of not only the House but state legislatures and governors' mansions across the country. Back from the dead, newly empowered Republicans promptly went about gerrymandering the shit out of the country, crushing labor unions, and passing even more onerous voting restrictions.

Because Democrats gave up on transformational policies that would have galvanized their voting base and the legion of young volunteers who had sweat and bled to put Obama in office, barely anyone came out to stop the onslaught of sociopathic puppy-mill owners and drunk-driving stepdads that made up the freshman GOP class of 2011. The obstructionist House shut down the government, leading to an unprecedented downgrade of the United States' credit rating. Voters rewarded Republicans' inveterate disrespect of the Process by giving them control of the Senate.

Thanks to the GOP's lock on the House, the once-transformative Obama spent his last six years in office as a technocratic dud. He was still capable of some (transient) good deeds: he mandated vital protections for immigrants and LGBT individuals and instituted a moratorium on the deportation of the most telegenic undocumented immigrants via executive order. At the same time, he vastly increased the scope and brutality of our security state and mass-surveillance apparatus, putting the Democratic imprimatur on the most depraved excesses of the Bush administration. In the liberal mind, this was okay. Sure, setting a precedent for extrajudicial murder of American citizens is a little wild; committing to drone warfare in a dozen or so countries after running on a peace platform is a touch much; funding Al Qaeda in Syria and Libya is a stretch; and expanding mass surveillance and imprisoning whistleblowers is not, as the kids say, a good look. But there were editorials lightly criticizing the president in the *New Republic* (purchased in 2012 by a Facebook oligarch whose husband used it as a springboard to buying a congressional seat), so surely this was an improvement over the stifling groupthink of the Bush years. Score one for liberal democracy.

In any event, making the civil rights of millions contingent on a guarantee from the White House, expanding the imperial presidency, and presiding over a tentacular surveillance state so high-key thicc it would have made Ceaușescu cum made a lot of sense so long as there would always be a Democratic hand at the till. Yes, they lost Congress and over a thousand seats in state legislatures, but thanks to demographic shifts and a booming stock market, Democrats had a 100 percent ironclad lock on the presidency, as evinced by Obama's convincing back-to-back victories. There was absolutely, categorically, utterly no chance a Republican could ever, ever, ever possibly take control of the White House ever again, insofar as doing so would require winning such solidly Democratic states as Michigan, Wisconsin, Ohio, Iowa, Pennsylvania, and Florida, all of which would remain in the Democratic column for eternity. Now let's all take a big sip of coffee at the Javits Center and read the 2016 election results . . .

Oh No

Ah, jeez. Oh boy. Yikes. It seems the human culmination of American liberalism lost to a senile (alleged!) rapist game show host. Welp. Pobody's nerfect, as the old saying goes.

Dear reader, we will not be so disingenuous as to say we predicted Donald Trump's victory. To be perfectly honest, we, too, assumed the Democrats' obviously patronizing bullshit would outweigh the clear and present danger to everyone's life. And, in fact, it was not a surge of blood-and-soil nationalism that made everyone look like assholes after they posted their prediction maps but merely the same people who always show up for Republicans doing what they always do against a discouraged, disinterested, and disenfranchised Democratic coalition. Republican voters were offered everything they had ever wanted—a new era of brutality and the repudiation of the symbol of Obama—while Democrats were served up four more years of morally incoherent and procedurally feckless liberalism. It was the logical conclusion, and the facts sure as shit didn't care about anyone's feelings.

The New Paranoid Style

The meanest thing you can say about liberalism (to a liberal, anyway) is that it's not really a set of beliefs. The values liberals *think* they own were always historically borrowed from the Left—e.g., racial equality, which American Communists agitated for *way* before mainstream libs, or women's and LGBT rights, which the Bolsheviks legalized while US liberals were still coming up with new sodomy laws and barring women from voting.

Beyond those values—which liberals tend to commercialize and monetize anyway—the rest of liberalism is just a system for managing capitalism. It's a collection of political and social norms that safely discharge the chaos generated by capital through gradual reform.

In good times—say, the postwar heyday of American manufacturing—this system gives the approximation of functionality (if you weren't a black, nonunion worker). But hit a profit squeeze like we did in the 1970s and liberalism will just as quickly dump the working class, press "start" on a bipartisan algorithm to break union power, and ctrl+alt+delete half a century's worth of wealth redistribution. The predictable result is a disillusioned and depoliticized populace plucking through the wreckage—people who either check out of electoral politics completely or turn toward the siren call of thuggish reaction.

A generation after the neoliberal turn, the Democratic Party, headed and staffed by self-professed liberals, is arguably to the right of Nixon on most economic issues and committed to a largely symbolic (and almost always negotiable) progressive cultural agenda to mask it. All that can really be expected of a Democratic government at this point is that it won't appoint another member of Opus Dei to the Supreme Court. Democrats' lack of vision suggests a historical descent into an also-ran party, one whose best shot at the

White House is to stumble through the door after whatever grotesque catastrophe befalls the country thanks to Republican governance. But this party will never—and can never—fundamentally change American politics.

Many liberals hold out some vestigial loyalty to the Democratic Party because they're the only thing protecting us from something even worse. But guess what? They're not even doing that anymore.

This is where we are now: American liberals have spent their *entire lives* focusing on norms, rules, and processes. They've chortled at the wacky radicals to their left and conducted the science of the possible, operating on what is "realistic," the only meaningful political value. In so doing, the Carter and Clinton administrations jettisoned a fair share of liberal principles: Yikes, did we shaft unions and sign health care over to insurance companies? Sorry, we were busy "getting things done," like deregulating the financial sector and ballooning the war on drugs.

The twenty-first century hasn't changed libs. Once the infamous third-world Marxist Obama got into office (thanks to a campaign that denounced war, racism, and the superrich), liberals didn't balk at his betrayals as president. They embraced his realistic positions, like protecting Wall Street after an epochal public looting and massively expanding a War on Terror that will now last 150 years. And then, in 2016, came über-realistic candidate Hillary, who had the best résumé—the most qualified candidate ever!—while mayo boy Bernie Sanders promised things he couldn't deliver, which were too left-wing to win a general election anyway.

And what happened? Fact-checked, focus-grouped, data-driven Clinton lost to the most deranged presidential candidate ever: a clown, a fraud, a sexual predator, an inveterate liar who has faked every single thing he's ever done—a giant cube of flesh who embodies all our vilest instincts and our ludicrous celebrity culture. She lost—the Democrats lost, the liberals lost—to *him*.

And then what did the liberals do? They all went insane, turned away from reality, denied the results of their poisoned politics. They bought every James Bond movie on Amazon, streamed them all at once, jumped into the bathtub, and emerged with epileptic visions of Putin chasing Hillary in an Aston Martin through Mexico City.

No one has divorced him- or herself from reality more swiftly than the post–2016 election American liberal. The levelheaded purveyors of reason, facts, and data have all become the inmates of the Magic Mountain. The Trump presidency invalidates their entire worldview. They're humiliated and discredited. They've been left wandering the hallways of an institution in a dirty bathrobe, zonked on Haldol and muttering about "active measures" and "dezinformatsiya."

Over fifty years after shit-lib par excellence Richard Hofstadter wrote the foundational text of American liberalism, "The Paranoid Style in American Politics," the essay needs a big fucking footnote: for decades, this country's liberal thinkers, politicians, and columnists have coasted on the basic truth of Hofstadter's writing—that American conservatism is a slapstick crew of loopy, bug-eyed, toxic conspiracy theorists, a carnival of souls either grasping for some glorious bygone era or living in a completely alternate universe out of a bad spy novel, with Russians and Communists hiding behind every corner.

The proudest liberals have now checked into that same asylum. Log on to Twitter or turn on MSNBC or read the *New York Times*; you'll get Infowars-level theories about how Trump, Sanders, left-wing podcasts, and even fucking mass shootings are all likely the work of the Kremlin. The libs have gazed into the abyss and punctured the membrane of their psyches. Now they spend their days barking into the void, punching out a Möbius strip of tweets and blog posts, safe inside their own heads, safe from the world that their dull, smug, dead-end politics have wrought. It's a long way from Roosevelt overseeing a vast new empire of enlightenment. After almost a century of tut-tutting the Left and the Right, the paranoid style has flipped: liberals are the cranks now.

And to them, we'll quote once more from the wisdom of *No Country For Old Men*'s Anton Chigurh, delivered in his final moments with a cornered, deluded victim: "You should admit your situation. There would be more dignity in it."

Taxonomies

Epic-Rant Dad

Epic-Rant Dad can be found throughout the American suburbs and on the outskirts of major cities, attending his kids' soccer games on his allotted weekends and filling Facebook with daily Adderall-induced missives about the fate of the Republic. His natural habitat is samba-themed marriage counseling and other fun things couples can do together. Unlike the more traditional, conservative American dad types, Epic-Rant Dad is not identified *only* by his love of American values and symbols (football, baseball, the Normandy landings, and other sports he wished he could have taken part in) but also by his insistence that liberals such as himself are the *true* patriots who fought and *won* the Cold War.

Once a die-hard Clintonite—watching Bill playing the sax on *Arsenio* taught him how to be cool—the Epic-Rant Dad has become, in the age of Trump, a patriotic crusader fighting to defend the Republic against the Slavic hordes. He accomplishes this by posting. He replies to Trump's tweets with "Hey, Cheeto Benito, is this the fake news you've been complaining about? #TheLiesAreComingFrom InsideTheHouse" and uploads videos of Kirsten Gillibrand's speeches to PornHub so viewers might jerk off a different organ: their brain. Epic-Rant Dad knows the names of all his teenage daughter's friends. Epic-Rant Dad brews his own beer on the weekends and names it things like "Fake News Alternative Ale," "Have You No Shame? Lager," and "Sir? Sir? Sir? Sir? Pilsner."

FIGHTING STYLE: Logic-based pragmatic brawler

SEXUAL REPRESSION LEVEL: "Hillary is the most qualified candidate in American history"

KISSINGER
MICRO-BREW BIBLE
100 BEST CHORD CHANGES OF 1972
BILL OF RIGHTS
LAKEVIEW GIRLS LACROSSE COACH OF THE YEAR
CREENWRITING SECRETS
ONLINE GRADUATE WITH HONORS
I CAN HAS MY DEMOCRACY BACK?
"When you get to the end of your rope, tie a knot and hang on." -FDR
LIFEQUOTE.COM
A small thing I like to call valor, Sir. (1286/x)
GIF
Tweet

Blue-Collar Democrat [Extinct]

The Blue-Collar Democrat was a medium- to large-sized flightless mammal discovered on Long Island in the 1930s and declared extinct less than a century later. The Blue-Collar Democrat inhabited both urban and rural areas, consuming a diet rich in meat and starch. Skeletal reconstructions show that it possessed a large body, stubby arms, a small tail, short legs, and a large, poofy hat with a rude saying written on the front. The hairs of the Blue-Collar Democrat were usually gray/black in color, while its most distinctive feature was a placid expression of general contentment.

Conservation efforts in the 1970s failed, due in large part to President Jimmy Carter's unwillingness to support key factors of the Blue-Collar's ecosystem: unions, rising wages, and jobs in general. Some scholars maintain that a certain number of Blue-Collar Democrats did not completely die out but instead evolved into either apathetic non-voters or paranoid, racist Republicans.

NATURAL PREDATORS: Industry and finance capital, debt collectors, the Democratic Party

LIFESTYLE: Family pass to the World's Fair

1932-1979
JOE
SIXPACK
WHITES
ONLY

Celebrity Dumbass

It's a well-known conservative tactic to attack liberals for hating—or insufficiently loving—the troops. But if those lizard-brained Rethuglicans had a clue, they would realize the American lib is a stalwart supporter of a different kind of soldier: the Celebrity Dumbass. At first glance, they cut a very different figure from the traditional military grunt, lacking the camouflage and jarhead chic. But look closer: Who stands on the front lines every day, eviscerating the forces of evil and tyranny? Who embodies the very best of us? Who fights for the soul of America and defends those who cannot defend themselves? If the conservative's fantasy of power is lighting up an Iraqi village with depleted uranium shells, the liberal's vision is an epic mic-drop moment from Meryl Streep or Jared Leto that instructs the president to check his privilege—and his dang toupee.

The highest tier of the Celebrity Dumbass officer corps is, of course, the Political Comedian. More than any other entertainers, they bring the fight straight to the enemy: the Bill Mahers, Sam Bees, and John Olivers of this world use the power of late-night comedy to beat back the hypocrisy, malice, and just plain derp of the American right wing, which is how the Democratic Party managed to soundly defeat a bumbling game show host running for president in 2016.

With each viral clip of epic evisceration, the Celebrity Dumbass preserves your freedom to consume their latest Pixar rom-com produced for tax purposes. You *want* them on that Facebook wall; you *need* them on that Facebook wall.

SUPERPOWERS: Charisma, remarkably low thetan levels

ALLIES: William Morris Endeavor, ICM

Allstate
Capital One
verizon
Raytheon
The Weinstein Company

Liberal Hawk

The horrors of the world are unavoidable. But while most of us look at those horrors and say "I like that" or "That's good; keep going," there are a brave few who boldly declare that things are bad and we must "do something." And if the evil actor in question happens to oppose America's imperial goals, there you will find the Liberal Hawk, bravely crying for nonspecific action.

Don't confuse the Liberal Hawk with its cousin, the Neocon. Sure, they may advocate the exact same policy goals of vague "American leadership" and push for the same confrontation with Iran and funding for any group from Ukraine's Hitler Appreciation Club to Syria's Jabhat al-Cumshit irredentist militias, so long as they "undermine Putin" and "advance democracy," and yes, their livelihoods are funded by magazines no one reads and think tanks that benefit no one but their murky Gulf sheikh and robber-baron descendants—but they're completely different. For one, the Liberal Hawk won't rail against safe spaces and PC culture the way the Neocon will. In one breath, the Liberal Hawk will quote a potential six-figure death toll from a potential intervention as "a price worth paying," then in the next be moved nearly to tears while describing to you the last book they read, which is invariably called something like *The Balls to Be a Woman: Golda Meir's War against Toxic Masculinity.*

But like all things, this comes down to compensation: while the Neocon is usually a fudge-fingered treat addict who can be bought off by any lobby so long as they bring snacks, the Liberal Hawk requires things like dry Riesling, ski holidays in Gstaad, and tickets for shit like "A Jazz Tribute to NATO."

FIGHTING STYLE: LinkedIn posts, cluster bombs

SEXUAL REPRESSION LEVEL: Offers free foot rubs to IDF soldiers

The Atlantic
IRAN
NOW?
...OR NEVER
love trumps hate.

App-hole

The App-hole rose from humble beginnings as a deeply antisocial college freshman to become one of the richest people alive. He earned billions coming up with a fun, cool, and free way for us to share our thoughts, locations, faces, blood types, secrets, lies, and weaknesses with corporate and governmental third parties. He parlayed his hatred and fear of his fellow human beings into a cybernetic work ethic and never-ending drive to leave the "meat-space" behind and become a cloud-based immortal entity.

The App-hole has ushered in a new and revolutionary form of American corporate culture in which you can dress like a teenager in the office, play Skee-Ball, ride a skateboard, and, most important, never leave the work compound. Following his first IPO, he redesigned his entire biology: installing hair, purchasing a personal trainer, and getting the secret kind of sex-enhancement surgery only rich people know about. After a rough period of bad press for statements like "Women don't have the proper skill stack to make equal pay" and "We need to modernize our age-of-consent laws," the App-hole has recently showed stirrings of a social conscience by investing billions into implanting a Fitbit into the neck of every African child. He hopes someday to totally eliminate the obsolete operating systems of unions, education, and public sanitation. The App-hole can currently be found one-upping the *Challenger* disaster with his private space program.

FUTURE DISRUPTIONS: Moon colony for breeding pairs, Plasmr: Connecting Blood Pods with the Marketplace, self-succing car, the White House

SKILL STACK: Wastes no energy by recycling all fecal matter into edible slurry

H-1B
amazon
H-1B
amazon
HEMO-GLOBE™
BETA
BLOOD ORIGIN:
EUROPEAN 91%
ASIAN 9%
[AFRICAN: 0%]

Wine Mom

Wine Mom's political evolution closely tracks that of her hero and Life Goals Inspiration Board avatar, Hillary Clinton: a baby boomer from a deeply conservative background who ended up in a bad marriage and found liberal politics after her divorce. About two years ago she realized that black people *might* have some legitimate complaints about the police after a lifetime of rolling up her windows while driving through "urban" neighborhoods. Now woke, she broadcasts her deep feelings of contempt for anyone who "centers whiteness" or "does erasure." Despite this, Wine Mom can most easily be found anywhere in the center of whiteness, erasing anyone who won't let her speak to their manager.

Wine Mom loves her SB (sauvignon blanc) and happy pills (Xanax, Percs, Ativan, etc.) and hates young people of any kind. Wine Mom's most trenchant critiques of the president come from her precocious children, whom she's always overhearing saying things like "Doesn't the pwesident know that the individual mandate shores up the insuwance market?" and "Mommy, Susan Sawandon is a big dumb poopyhead who wants Twump to be her boyfwiend."

FIGHTING STYLE: Calling out cultural appropriation via GIFs of black women

FINISHING MOVE: Shade, side-eye, clapback

Corporate Feminist

The Corporate Feminist is dedicated to ensuring equal representation and equal pay for all women who are C-suite executives at major corporations. Indeed, the boardrooms of companies like Union Carbide, Exxon, Lockheed Martin, and Country-Wide have been boys' clubs for too long, and it's long past time for women to get their due. You see, if the corporate culture of the pharmaceutical, defense, health insurance, and tech industries more accurately reflected the gender makeup of the country they rule, they would be softer and more caring, nurturing, and ruthlessly efficient, just like women.

She's dedicated to making sure her male groundskeepers do their fair share of the emotional labor she demands of her nannies. All the Sherpas on her Nepalese estate are given copies of *Lean In.* You can catch a glimpse of the Corporate Feminist as you walk through the first-class cabin of the airplane, but *do not* make eye contact.

VEHICLE OF CHOICE: Last surviving African elephant

LATEST PATENT PENDING: Blood test that determines Myers-Briggs type within five seconds

STRONGER
TOGETHER

Movie Blob

The Movie Blob is a pop-culture obsessive who filters all his political beliefs and interpersonal behavior through the prism of films, comic books, television shows, and video games. As a result, he is deeply invested in crafting politics from submental drivel created for children. This creates ideological complications when studios end up buying him off with limited-edition action figures, thereby forcing him to drastically revise his past statements about the *Batman vs. Superman* nineteen-hour director's cut.

This man-child-man sees himself as part of a small group of social outcasts imbued with incredibly cool powers who fight to protect the very people who shun and persecute them. The Movie Blob insists that he's one of the "good" mutants and not the kind that uses their encyclopedic knowledge of pop-culture marginalia for evil. He is constantly on the lookout for ways to distinguish himself from his opposite on the right—YouTube Atheist Logic Guy, the bad kind of nerd who hates women because of his deeply stunted sexuality.

The Movie Blob instead writes think pieces like "Video: Black Widow OBLITERATES Misogyny" and "Let's Get Real: Lara Croft's Boobs are TOO Big." He has argued that if the members of the Galactic Senate had all been women, the Empire never would have invaded Naboo. But, like any true fan of graphic novels, he understands that the world isn't as simple as good vs. evil, and the line between hero and villain is sometimes blurred. Therefore, he's open and honest about the multiple restraining orders filed against him by the patrons and organizers of Dragoncon '06.

FAVORITE POLITICAL THINKERS: Bane, the Joker, Rorschach, Spider-Man's uncle

FAVORITE POLITICAL IDEOLOGIES: The Force, the Assassin's Creed, that thing Spock does with his hand

ALLY
Suspiria
Blu-ray Disc
SEX OFFENDER

(Intermission)

THE CALL OF NEOLIBERALISM: A BRIEF HISTORY

"Neoliberal" is a term that gets thrown around a lot these days without much concern for context or accuracy, much less the hurt it causes. Kids are coming home from school confused and frightened because they were called "neolibs" on the playground. Too many parents are being forced to have "the talk" about what it means to be market-friendly with their Codys and Jennaphers at too young an age.

On its face, it sounds like something good. "Neo," meaning the hero of the Matrix films, and "liberal," meaning someone who wishes things were good instead of bad. Surely the advent of some kind of new and powerful liberal like this would be a cause for celebration, right?

You'd think so, but in today's parlance, it's a term of abuse hurled at respected opinion columnists that the vulgar Marxist "Left" regards as too damn reasonable.

Broadly speaking, neoliberalism is a political and ideological project that gained traction in the 1970s across the Western world that sought to return to the laissez-faire roots of "classical" or "economic" liberalism; it aimed to curtail the gains made by labor in the twentieth century and to restore upper-class power through "free" markets and unregulated capital.

But it went even further than the classical gas: traditional, classical liberals might say that one must not interfere with the economy—one *could* do it, but one shouldn't, because it's bad. The *neo* half of the neoliberal idea insists that one *can't* interfere with the economy. As in, it's not possible; science has proven it. It's a thing outside of human control, beyond time and the wall of sleep. All we can do is sacrifice in the market's name.

We can trace the origins of this ideology to a meeting of economists, philosophers, and business leaders organized by Friedrich Hayek at Colorado's historic Overlook Hotel in 1947. Seeing a Western world devastated by the horrors of World War II, the labor movement, robust welfare states, and a population with too much free time, Hayek knew he had to do something.

That something became known simply as the Overlook Society. This group sought to promote a frank and productive exchange of views on how best to preserve market competition and private property in a world full of increasingly willful children in need of harsh correction. This fairly raucous affair was marked by vigorous debate and even more vigorous partying, such as when Nobel Prize winner Milton Friedman entertained guests by dressing in an assless bear costume and performing a raunchy version of his famous "Pencil" lecture by making several no. 2's "disappear."

Through their conferences and writings, the Overlook Society laid the groundwork for a reinvigorated philosophy of economic liberalism, as well as a renewed spiritual interest in certain long-forgotten Babylonian deities among American and European elites.

Later in the 1970s, future Supreme Court justice Lewis F. Powell Jr. laid another cornerstone of the neoliberal revolution with his Powell Memo. One of the all-time great memos, Powell urged politicians and business leaders to become more involved in fighting back against a new "Attack on the American Free Enterprise System." Powell was responding to a nascent consumer rights movement represented by Ralph Nader and his seminal exposé of General Motors, *Murder Mobile: Your Car Will Fucking Decapitate You*.

A former corporate lawyer who sat on the board of Philip Morris, Powell knew better than most the threat to freedom posed by increasing public awareness that people's lives were incidental to the bottom line. The Powell Memo forcefully argued that capital needed its own collective project to fight back against haters like Ralph Nader and the working class. In a war of ideas, Powell understood that his side needed to tool up, and that think tanks would be the trenches of the front lines.

Through a huge influx of corporate money, organizations like the Manhattan Institute and the Heritage Foundation were set up to promote this ideology as well as the esoteric rites and rituals of the Overlook Society, and to craft policies designed to nourish the vast and ancient elder gods they worshipped.

The essential question the neoliberal revolution sought to address was: What are human beings for? And what is the best way to serve man? Are individuals each creative and self-determined beings best served by acting in concert to exercise democratic control over the economic and political systems they live under? Or are they best served by acting as faceless nodes competing against one another in a massive orgone-harvesting project designed to fulfill the Redeemer prophecy as foretold in the works of the mad Arab Abdul Alhazred, given new and abominable life by the Overlook Society?

If you're reading this book in one of the few "free" moments you have, on your way to a job that's slowly sapping your will to live, you already know that the good side won.

In other words, neoliberalism is the guiding ideology of economic thought, political management, and occult magik of our times, and as such it is impossible to define. Though it accurately describes the policies pursued by every American president since Jimmy Carter, it's essentially unnameable and indescribable. No one really knows what it means, and it is precisely because the term is so hard to define that it's such an effective and poisonous epithet.

When one uses a term like *neoliberal* to describe people who support free markets, foreign intervention, and the dismantling of the traditional welfare state, one removes humanity and agency from a diverse group of individuals and the ancient and secret religion they belong to. Think about that the next time you decide to drop the n-bomb.

Perhaps the single greatest feature of neoliberalism is that it's entirely compatible with contemporary values of racial and sexual equality, provided they don't stray too far into *income* equality. The children of the Overlook Society are overwhelmingly pro–gay rights, pro–women's rights, pro–civil rights, etc. And why wouldn't they be? Being tolerant, outwardly friendly, and socially liberal makes waging outright class warfare and pursuing the secret worship of vast and ancient alien races that much easier.

What's more, how could a term that applies equally to Democrats *and* Republicans mean anything? If it accurately describes the horizon of possibility offered by *both* options available in American politics, then why do the two parties oppose each other so much? Why even have elections?

Since they're more efficient and rational than the thin sliver of consciousness that sits atop the abyssal depths of the individual human mind, why not just let markets determine our individual worth? If all our lives are in fact governed by forces that are so essentially inscrutable and beyond our control that they cannot even be named, what hope do we have but a blissful retreat into madness?

Furthermore, if a word doesn't really have a meaning, then how can one oppose the concept it represents? The answer is one can't, and one shouldn't try! Ph'nglui mglw'nafh R'lyeh wgah'nagl fhtagn!

CHAPTER THREE

CONS

To be conservative, then, is to prefer the familiar to the unknown, to prefer the tried to the untried, fact to mystery, the actual to the possible, the limited to the unbounded, the near to the distant, the sufficient to the superabundant, the convenient to the perfect, present laughter to utopian bliss.

—**Michael Oakeshott**

In today's America, being a proud virgin is no easy task.

—**Ben Shapiro**

he right wing in America is like Dracula: a grotesque avatar of inherited wealth who is unkillable, casts no reflection in mirrors, and lives off the blood of peasants. Ever since the modern conservative movement was birthed from William F. Buckley Jr.'s unholy womb, the American Right has mutated into more and more grotesque forms, reaching its logical apex in the election of Donald Trump. As of this writing, right-wingers control every branch of government with only about 30 percent of the country actually supporting them. After conservatives sat humiliated on the sidelines for the first half of the twentieth century, the apparition of St. Reagan in 1979 restored ancient conservative rule, standing athwart history yelling "Stop!" at black voters and anyone trying to obtain affordable health care. To be a modern-day conservative means you think golf is fun, cigars are cool, and wearing a suit every day is a fascinating hobby.

Who are these people? And how can they possibly be defeated?

Even though the standard American lib might desire many of the same "good" things as you and I, their politics have a congenital defect that makes them easy marks for capital and empire. Their problem is not only their beliefs but also their lack of conviction. Conservatives, on the other hand, have no such void at their core. They know what they want, and they have a political vision for how to get it. The problem is simply that what they want is all *bad*. To put it another way, America's liberals are the good cops. They appear in viral videos in which they play basketball with diverse teens, participate in charity bike races, and look the other way only on evidence-planting and extrajudicial murder. Conservatives are the bad cops, right down to their Oakley shades, strained to the breaking point as they wrap around their fat, pink heads.

In what passes for conservatives' moral vision, they embody all the worst demons of Protestantism and capitalism. They're the living, breathing id of hierarchy and oppression. A descendant of America's Calvinist tradition, modern secular conservatism exists to settle the same pinched-faced hysterics into a comfortable and pampered suburban existence. Despite its religious affectations, conservatism long ago replaced God with country, which allows them to directly worship America as both their lord and personal friend while celebrating the same petty and punitive characteristics that defined an earlier deity. To the conservative, America's vast wealth and power are signs of its goodness, because if there's one thing the Bible is clear about in both the Old and New Testaments, it's that rich and powerful empires are good and blessed by God.

So what does "America" mean to a conservative? What do they really believe in? The answer to both questions is, of course:

freedom. America is a shining beacon of freedom, with a hype man called "liberty." It's the best country because it's the freest country, and, as such, the greatest country that God—which is also America—ever created. A liberal will most likely snort at this, cough up their kombucha, fall off their tassled-handlebarred bicycle, and get up off the pavement just long enough to say that conservatives have traditionally been violently opposed to the freedom of *most* people in American history. They would be right, but are, as usual, missing the more important point, which is that, to a conservative, *freedom* means something very different from what a normal person imagines.

In the right-wing vernacular, *freedom* means the freedom to exercise one's God-given right to dominate anyone deemed lower than you. This includes rich over poor, men over women, employers over employees, white over black, and America over the rest of the world. This is why, in the conservative mythology, there are few greater enemies than "big government." In the modern era, it's usually the federal government that has unjustly intervened in this natural order.

During the George W. Bush years, Thomas Frank asked in his book *What's the Matter with Kansas?* why average, salt-of-the-earth types consistently vote for a party so transparently dedicated to fucking them over. The answer given by liberals is usually that the conservative movement is running a massive grift wherein they trick their marks into voting against their own economic interests by catering to their prejudices through a number of "social" issues and culture-war signifiers like abortion and gay marriage. In other words, conservatives run on gays, guns, and God as they dismantle the public sector and facilitate the upward transfer of wealth once they get into office.

While it's true that anyone who's not a millionaire or richer is voting against their economic interests by supporting Republicans, the same could be said of the modern Democratic Party as well, and this idea that the Republican base is being "tricked" lets them off the hook too easily. Enough of the red-state rubes in question *might* vote against economic domination if the Democrats offered an alternative, but in the absence of that, liberals would do well to realize that, to the traditionally minded, the maintenance of racial, religious, and gender hierarchies does, in fact, deliver the goods to the roughly one-third of this country that identifies as conservative. They *do* get something tangible from this deal: resistance against bathroom sickos, the petty privilege of being white, and the cathartic sadism of American military conquest and warfare.

Conservative religion holds that the representatives of that sadism, its prophets, are the tough, stoic heirs to America's rugged frontier tradition. But the collection of penguin-shaped dunces in Under Armour polos and khaki shorts grazing through America's exurbs tends to spoil this myth. These war-dads and bow-tie perverts are unable to reconcile their actual lives with the values of primitive domination and masculine authority they hold so dear. This dynamic is best embodied by political philosopher, neocon godfather, and genuine Harvard professor of "manliness" Harvey Mansfield, who once told the *New York Times* he displays his own strength and masculine prowess by "lifting things" and "opening things" for his wife, "who is quite small." Mansfield noted that his lifting included "furniture. Not every night, but routinely." *

* Deborah Solomon, "Of Manliness and Men," *New York Times Magazine*, March 12, 2006.

Since the noble qualities conservatives obsess over have been bureaucratized out of existence in the "civilized" West, they fetishize military "operators," cowboys, and business entrepreneurs, imagining themselves to be rebelling against modern culture. Unbearable, treacly self-regard gives them a lump in their throat when they think of parades, the flag, baseball, and other people running into machine-gun fire on D-Day. Books with names like *The Patriot's Playbook* and *American Lion: How to Thrive in Life after Marriage* sit on their nightstands. Their lives are the epitome of the much-derided "safe space," and they are constantly offended by everyone and everything who ever hurt their feelings or, even worse, hurt the feelings of America.

Ironically, becoming a popular *movement* is precisely what undermined the right-wing project drawn up by its founding intellectuals: guys like William Buckley and Russell Kirk—names that no conservative will know in fifty years—planned to build a Platonic kingdom of logical, limited government that funneled society's wealth to deserving aristocrats, where intellectuals would become philosopher kings over the simple masses. But that required popularizing their ideology and mobilizing the hoopleheads to win elections, which in turn required a much more rigorous apparatus of power and propaganda than the Republicans of old.

Over time, supported by the money of anemic oligarchs who saw the potential to rubber-stamp their (fairly nonideological) capital accumulation, the conservative brainiacs and think-tankers preached culture war, states' rights, small government, and low taxes. They smuggled in right-wing economics, something middle America didn't care about, by draping it in cultural bullshit, something middle America couldn't get enough of. And, as Frank's book argued, it played pretty well. For a long time they masterfully triangulated racial and class resentments to enrich the upper classes while the Democrats gave up trying to offer alternatives. Within a couple of decades, the New Deal was dying, and "conservatism" was back, with an ideology, a coalition, presidents in office, and a vast customer base—er, voter base—of angry, aging white cranks.

Only problem was, by opening the doors to the CHUDs and the riffraff, the Republicans let in a bunch of wackjobs who *actually believed* the intellectuals' Noble Lie, or at least pretended to in order to out-crazy an increasingly batshit wave of GOP populists. As the years rolled on, the movement's homophobia, racism, and authoritarianism started to unnerve even the very ghouls who set the whole thing in motion.

The Republican Party has certainly conquered American politics. The catch, however, is that in the meantime, American *culture* could not be more inhospitable to them. The monster created by the effete intellectuals may now turn against its masters. Donald Trump is a stupid, gauche, uncultured philistine whose unabashed jingoism and racism has probably inaugurated a new era of right-wing Blood and Soil politics—which, believe it or not, hinders the interests of the well-manicured, multinational cartel of rich Republican vampires that nurtured the conservative movement.

Now, before we forecast where that nightmare project is ultimately headed, let's meet some of those aforementioned philosopher kings and queens who founded this dark universe.

Conservatism: A Rich Intellectual Tradition

Like any good political movement, American conservatism draws on its own tradition of writers and thinkers that make it vital, complex, and, most important, *extremely* fucking funny. Despite being caricatured as less of an ideology than a series of "irritable mental gestures," "the incessant whining of collicky adult babies," or "thinly veiled justifications for base prejudice and ignorance," the conservative movement does have a proud intellectual heritage of hating anything intellectual. Great minds like Ben Shapiro or Megan McArdle weren't just hatched as fully pupated geniuses—they were the inheritors of a long and storied conservative canon of truly impressive men and women who have shaped the world we live in today.

Russell Kirk

"Who?" you're probably asking. And you would be right to do so. Russell Kirk hasn't been relevant to American conservatism since Gerald Ford last fell down a flight of stairs, but there are still some pencil-necks out there (mostly employed by the *New York Times* op-ed page) who will insist that "conservative" doesn't refer to goose-stepping neo-fascists and snake-handling religious fanatics. You've got it all wrong, they insist. Conservatism is a rich intellectual tradition!

To make the case, they can't point to the collection of televangelists, game show hosts, carnival barkers, and anime characters who inspire contemporary reactionary thought, so they dust off ol' Russ. Kirk was a grumpy Catholic paleocon who called automobiles "mechanical Jacobins" and whose books are filled with such sterling insights as "Tradition is good; that's why it's traditional" and "Christianity, gotta have it." The next time some bow-tied dingus brings up Russell Kirk after the speaker of the House proposes giving cops rocket launchers, remember that the last person to read Kirk was required to do so for David Brooks's Yale class about humility.

Jerry Falwell and Pat Robertson

The Master Blaster of rising theocracy, Falwell and Robertson spearheaded the radicalization of American evangelical Christians. Before this power duo came along, most God-touched citizens steered clear of political organizing and, in many cases, voting. "That's the devil's bidness," they would remark before returning to their humble beet harvest. It was only in the 1970s, when Big Government Liberals started interfering with their noble folkways, that evangelical Christians awakened politically.

No, it wasn't the Supreme Court's *Roe v. Wade* decision legalizing abortion that broke the camel's back. Common mistake. It was actually the federal government's efforts to strip tax-exempt status from segregated Christian private schools. Something had to be done to stop this godless assault on traditional values. Jerry Falwell, who'd founded a radio show called the *Old-Time Gospel Hour and Klanbake* as a youth and spent the 1950s and '60s barnstorming against integration, founded the Moral Majority in 1979 to protest the loss of Bob Jones University's tax exemption for the "crime" of forbidding black students from attending. He was helped in his mission by Pat Robertson, another Baptist fire-eater whose *700 Club* show kept generations of Christian shut-ins company while they wrote outraged letters to PBS about Henrietta Pussycat's whorish ensembles.

These Pentecostal Powerhouses combined to turn the 1980s into the decade when white Christians woke up to the necessity of fighting the culture war at the ballot box. Along the way, Falwell sued Larry Flynt for writing that he fucked his sister, resulting in a landmark Supreme Court decision that has freed trolls to own the shit out of public figures with no consequences ever since.

Robertson actually ran for president in the Republican primary in 1988, but lost to human charisma volcano George H. W. Bush. In later years Falwell and Robertson both presided over religious colleges that spit out class after class of glassy-eyed true believers who filled the ranks of the W. Bush administration. The Bush years were also the high point for Robertson's and Falwell's most insane public statements: blaming 9/11 on feminists, blaming Hurricane Katrina on voodoo, and defending Liberian dictator Charles Taylor (who awarded Robertson a gold-mining concession in his country). Robertson also touted a pancake mix that he claimed gave him the ability to leg press two thousand pounds.

Ayn Rand

In the pantheon of great Russian novelists, names like Dostoyevsky, Gogol, Turgenev, Tolstoy, and Bulgakov spring to mind. Missing from the usual suspects is Rand, whose catalog is richer than that of all those goofies put together. Perhaps the single greatest popularizer of the "libertarian" strain of right-wing thought, Ayn Rand immigrated to America in 1926 after the Bolshevik Revolution and immediately began her own American success story. She traveled to Hollywood with dreams of being a screenwriter, and a chance meeting with Cecil B. DeMille scored her the role of "Jewess #2" in the biblical epic *The King of Kings.* She went on to write a batshit manual advising Hollywood studios on how best to glorify industrialists and stamp out Communism.*

> **Don't** preach the superiority of public ownership as such over private ownership. **Don't** preach or imply that all publicly-owned projects are noble, humanitarian undertakings by grace of the mere fact that they are publicly-owned—while preaching, at the same time, that private property or the defense of private property rights is the expression of some sort of vicious greed, of anti-social selfishness or evil. . . .
>
> Don't spit into your own face, or, worse, pay miserable little rats to do it.
>
> You, as a motion picture producer, are an industrialist. All of us are employees of an industry which gives us a good living. There is an old fable about a pig who filled his belly with acorns, then started digging to undermine the roots of the oak from which the acorns came. Don't let's allow that pig to become our symbol.

Despite her early success in Tinseltown, Rand didn't really become famous in America until she published *The Fountainhead,* her novel about an architect named Howard Roark who is

---

* Ayn Rand, "Screen Guide for Americans," The Motion Picture Alliance for the Preservation of American Ideals, 1947, http://archive.lib.msu.edu/DMC/AmRad/screenguideamericans.pdf.

better than everyone else. By creating a character who was supposed to be the coolest guy ever and who directly said all the things she believed, Rand took literature to a brave and bold new place. She would use this technique again in her magnum opus, *Atlas Shrugged,* a novel about a big, powerful train that also features a character who was the greatest person who ever lived and said exactly what Rand believed, sometimes for stretches of ninety pages, all of it shimmering prose.

Rand knew that before her arrival, art and fiction were mostly tools for the weak and desperate to blame others for their lot in life. A true revolutionary, she embedded in her fiction a competing philosophy, a holistic system of ethics, metaphysics, and aesthetics. She called this system "Objectivism," because it was objectively true. This system held that man is an inherently heroic being and that individual happiness and fulfillment is the only moral good one should aspire to. During a famous appearance on the game show *You Bet Your Life,* she told host Groucho Marx that Objectivism came only "out of my own mind, with the sole acknowledgment of a debt to Aristotle, the only philosopher who ever influenced me." To which Groucho retorted, "Try telling that to Nietzsche!" and then ashed his cigar in her lap.

Like all great philosophers, Rand realized that her system of ethics didn't mean anything unless she possessed a cadre of credulous rich people hanging off her every word. So, she created the Collective, a group of what the weak and timid usually call "friends," who would meet at her apartment to go over the latest draft of *Atlas* while Rand berated them for their many personal failings. A young Alan Greenspan was an early acolyte and member of the Collective who would go on to apply the Objectivist beliefs of anti-altruism and ethical megalomania to great effect as chairman of the Federal Reserve. In perhaps her most glorious philosophical triumph, Rand broke up the marriage of two members of the Collective so she could keep having sex with the guy using only reason, facts, and logic.

Rand's legacy in right-wing thought is clear. Not only did she write several thousand pages' worth of pseudo-philosophical drivel that declared the highest moral good was achieved in being the biggest asshole possible, but, in elevating reason as supreme among all human faculties, she was the first philosopher to elevate facts over feelings.

G. K. Chesterton

Gilbert Keith Chesterton is the favorite writer of a particular type of American reactionary: the Trad(itional)Cath(olic). He taught a generation of religious weirdos that piety can be funny and thoughtful and that wearing tarp-sized tweed jackets and a cape while carrying a walking stick is a cool look. Chesterton was Edwardian England's most eloquent advocate for distributism, a Catholic social and economic system that contemporary TradCaths embrace, more (skepticism of big-government socialism) or less (actually distributing anything to anyone). Like many of the Catholic Church's most ardent defenders, Chesterton was a convert, which made him directly opposed to the Church's fiercest critics and those heretics who actually had to grow up in it.

An extremely prolific writer, Chesterton was a poet, columnist, critic, and lay theologian who is best known for creating the famous character Encyclopedia Brown. A legendary wit, Chesterton is beloved by contemporary conservatives for his many deliciously quotable lines, such as "The worst part of being an educated man is receiving an education," "The thing I love most about writing is not writing," and "I owe my considerable girth to my beloved mother, who, when she sat around the house, sat *around* the house."

Unfortunately, his body of work and reputation as a beloved doddering fatso were undone when it came out that his writing inspired C. S. Lewis to believe in God and write a stilted and punishing fantasy series that ruined the tender minds of a generation of children. In addition to incessantly coining acerbic phrases, Chesterton also enjoyed other pastimes beloved by contemporary conservatives, such as civil debate, anti-Semitism, and sweating while he ate.

Paul Kersey

The original "liberal who got mugged by reality," Paul Kersey was a softhearted Upper West Sider whose heart bled for the poor and unfortunate until Jeff Goldblum and his gang of savage thugs brutally attacked his wife and daughter. Instead of checking his privilege or retreating to his safe space, Paul went out into the mean streets of Manhattan to deal out hot lead to thieves and vandals. This hard right turn mirrored much of American culture in the late 1970s and early '80s as liberal, soft-on-crime policies led to gang rule in the streets.

Tough on crime and strongly in favor of the Second Amendment, Kersey had a Death Wish for the criminals who endangered law-abiding American citizens and a Life Wish for Constitutional Liberty. He also once lit up an entire South Bronx neighborhood with a Browning .50 cal. That was awesome. Whenever you read the comments on a local news article about crime in which every other response is a guy fantasizing about burying hip-hop thugs up to their necks and driving a John Deere over them, you're taking part in the conservative style pioneered by Mr. Kersey.

Fred Flintstone

In the conservative worldview, the anchor of society is a strong father figure. All good things flow from a strong family unit, and you can't have one of those without a man who pays the bills and lays down the law. As the prototypical blue-collar guy and paterfamilias, Fred Flintstone was one of the first models of fatherly virtue. Fred was a lover of simple things: rock bowling, driving his rock car, drinking rock beer, and killing pterodactyls for fun.

Untainted by postmodern influences, Fred showed that things were better when the man was the head of the house. He belonged to fraternal organizations like the Water Buffalo Lodge and the John Bauxite Society, which encouraged civil leadership and homogeneous communities. Fred always insisted on ordering as many brontosaurus ribs as he wanted, regardless of Mayor Rockberg's whining that it was "too much" and would "tip his car over." Fred created an intellectual justification for wishing you lived in the distant past that conservatives have been cribbing from ever since.

William F. Buckley Jr.

The true godfather of modern conservatism, William Francis Buckley Jr. did more to advance the intellectual case for conservative principles than anyone else in the latter half of the twentieth century. He did all this despite being technically dead since the late seventies. As a writer, thinker, and social gadfly, Buckley remains an iconic figure on the right. He's still regarded as a great mind because he affected a toff accent and was on television a lot. He remains so beloved that even his darting, gila monster–like eyes and tongue are often described by writers even worse than he was as "energetic" or possessing a certain "twinkle." This impressive appearance made him a memorable party guest and a formidable opponent of civil rights.

Not much is known about Buckley's early life; he first appears as a member of Yale's Skull and Bones society, where he quickly rose to prominence by spending the longest time ever jacking off in a coffin. "I feel quite at home in here, Duckie!" he was once quoted as saying during a particularly successful initiation rite. Buckley's name does crop up again in the public record during his two years working as a professional snitch for the CIA in the fifties; however, it has long been speculated that he was a guinea pig in the Agency's infamous "Operation F.A.U.N.T.L.E.R.O.Y.," a Cold War–era mind-control program designed to create the most insufferably precious fancy lad of all time.

After emerging as a fully formed dandy from the Ivies and the Agency, Buckley got his start in politics as a lickspittle for Joe McCarthy and would go on to lend his name and every cliché he could muster to virtually every crackpot right-wing movement or group in America and every blood-drenched dictatorship overseas. He did this as the founder of the premier journal of conservative thought, the *National Review,* for which he penned classic lines such as "the White community in the South is entitled to take such measures as are necessary to prevail [over black people because] . . . it is the advanced race" and "Everyone detected with AIDS should be tattooed in the upper forearm, to protect common-needle users, and on the buttocks, to prevent the victimization of other homosexuals" and something to the effect of: I was dead wrong about apartheid in the American South back then but am correct about apartheid in South Africa now.

In both "life" and death, Buckley is often positioned against his great nemesis, Gore Vidal, whom he famously called a "qwee-ah!" on national television. The clash of these two titans of the Left and Right makes for an interesting contrast. On one hand you have Vidal, who produced a major body of work, including dozens of novels and plays and hundreds of essays touching on every aspect of American history, literature, and politics; on the other you have Buckley, who wrote a book about how there are too many Jews at Yale, a few lyrical essays about how much he loved sailing, and a series of spy novels in which a thinly veiled alter ego named Blackford Oakes fucks the queen of England. Vidal and Buckley's famous spat on television is also funny because it involved Buckley calling Vidal a homo and then threatening to beat him up in the gayest way possible.

Buckley died around 1977, but his shambling cadaver maintained a bizarre form of "un-life" until 2008, robotically churning out columns, making TV appearances, and taking young men sailing. His influence on the American Right is still deeply felt. While many people believe Buckley defined the parameters of the modern right wing, his *really* lasting contribution is the creation of a pretentious writing style aped by every single slob, moron, and dork to come out of a college Republican group and land bylines in Buckley's characteristically undead magazine.

Murray Rothbard and Hans-Hermann Hoppe

One of the many ways in which libertarianism is like Scientology is that both organizations try to ease new recruits in. Scientologists don't bring up Xenu and volcanoes full of dead aliens until one has already signed the trillion-year contract; they start with e-meters and diet tips. Similarly, when libertarians make their pitch to skeptical youth, they tend to emphasize the commonsense, "economics 101" writings of Milton Friedman and Friedrich Hayek. Capitalism is just choice! Everybody loves choice, right? It's only later, after one has hosted an awkward campaign fund-raiser for Bob Barr and named one's firstborn Bitcoin that they offer up the hard stuff.

Murray Rothbard and Hans-Hermann Hoppe took the fuzzy, freedom-loving logic of libertarianism to its logical endpoint, a place that most of the uninitiated would consider a nightmare of inhumanity. Rothbard, who didn't leave the island of Manhattan until his forties due to an intense fear of bridges and tunnels, realized that a political system based on property had a child problem: Children don't own property and they don't work, so what is the basis for their claim to rights? His answer was: they don't have one. Children are the property of their parents, who can dispose of them as they wish. They can't *kill* them, of course (that would violate the non-aggression principle), but they could starve them to death or, if they're angling for a trip to Branson, sell them.

For his part, Hoppe reached the conclusion—inescapable,

but unspoken by most mainstream libertarians—that democracy is incompatible with liberty. Property is the basis for freedom, so society is, obviously, a mutual agreement among property owners. All functions of the state should be privatized. What about people who don't own property? asks the nerd. They don't have rights, bitch, answers Hoppe. Hoppe argued that the most "natural" form of government was feudal aristocracy, and that the imposition of the taxation and redistribution associated with liberal democracy was in fact far worse than the serfdom of an earlier era. Hoppe's biggest idea was that because democracy is majoritarian by nature, the majority of people will choose to be protected from oppression and discrimination. This, to Hoppe, was why democracy is a terrible evil that must be abolished and replaced with a system of unfettered private tyrannies.

Often libertarians will couch their arguments in terms of personal freedom and sell them based on the idea that if we would only abolish the capital gains tax, the EPA, and public schools, we would all be much freer to be you and me. Once big government is out of the way, we can all smoke weed and fuck whatever our 3-D printers can dream up, so the argument goes. But for some reason, serious libertarians like Hoppe don't cotton to the notion that their politics are about expanding the personal freedom of other people, particularly young people and racial and sexual minorities. Hoppe correctly realized that the total abolition of the state in favor of a strict regime of private property and laissez-faire economics would involve the brutal curtailment of the freedoms of speech, movement, and bodily autonomy for the vast majority of people, and that was a good thing. He envisioned a society managed by a combination of large landowners, homeowners' associations, and insurance companies that would enforce the property rights of their customers and no one else's. What's more, Hoppe also realized that this society would necessarily involve the forced expulsion of anyone who thought differently. According to Hoppe:

> There can be no tolerance toward democrats and communists in a libertarian social order. They will have to be physically separated and expelled from society. Likewise, in a covenant founded for the purpose of protecting family and kin, there can be no tolerance toward those habitually promoting lifestyles incompatible with this goal. They—the advocates of alternative, non-family and kin-centered lifestyles such as, for instance, individual hedonism, parasitism, nature-environment worship, homosexuality, or communism—will have to be physically removed from society too, if one is to maintain a libertarian order.*

This is the kind of stuff that would send a normie running for the hills, but once you've bought your third Penn Jillette book, you're pot committed. If any intellectual has laid the groundwork for where the Right is headed now, it's Hoppe: scorched-earth libertarianism fueled by atavistic hatred of minorities, queers, and Communists.

---

* Hans-Hermann Hoppe, *Democracy—The God That Failed: The Economics and Politics of Monarchy, Democracy, and Natural Order* (New Brunswick, NJ: Transaction Publishers, 2001), 218.

Now let's depart from the mind castles of these great figures and witness modern conservatism in practice.

We're Openly, 100 Percent Evil: Conservatives Throughout American History

There was a time in the country when men were truly free—when rugged individuals could carve out and tame a piece of the American wilderness, build a home, buy some seed and some workers, and wring wealth from the black earth. A man's plantation was his castle. A man's wife was his lady. A man's slaves were his property. A man's hat was . . . I don't know, his daughter. The government existed to protect him from foreign invaders and domestic cutthroats, but otherwise had no power to interfere with his life and works. A man would wake up; spend the morning reading on his veranda being fanned by one of his cheerful thralls; ride his horse through his gorgeous fields of cotton and indigo; shoot anything that flew, walked, or crawled on his property; and have the cook serve it up to him at a sumptuous dinner. This was the real Land of Liberty.

Then, under a dark cloud, the bleeding-heart do-gooders of the nanny state invaded and ruined everything with their freedom-stifling bureaucracy and so-called Thirteenth Amendment just because some visionary liberty-lovers banded together to secede from the union to expand human slavery.

Nothing to Fear but Equality Itself

But the arc of history bends toward justice. Thankfully, the economics of war created opportunities for capital accumulation beyond the dreams of even the most successful antebellum agribusiness entrepreneur, creating a new class of Free Men: the slanderously named robber barons. These business titans used their massive wealth to push the boundaries of what freedom could mean. Yachts as big as mansions, mansions as big as hippodromes, days filled with oysters, champagne, and showgirls. You could hire Pinkertons to murder Irishmen, name libraries and concert halls after yourself, and get gout. Then, once again, big-government pencil-pushers, jealous of the robber barons' #successwin lifestyles, destroyed their freedom with the so-called New Deal, all just because unfettered capitalist speculation had destroyed the world's economy. This is how freedom dies—to thunderous applause.

After that, entire generations were lost—hooked and abused by the foul regulatory regime of FDR's shock troops. Gender and racial caste systems were thankfully maintained, but the laissez-faire freedom of the wild nineteenth century was replaced by a stultifying order of high taxes, strong unions, and restrained innovation—all because a solid majority of American voters came out of the Great Depression convinced that capitalism needed to be tightly controlled by government oversight! Cowards. So the nation's achievers and visionaries spent decades in the wilderness, scheming and theorizing about how to get regular schmoes to recognize that untrammeled economic liberty was in their best interests.

Captains of industry spent the 1950s exchanging samizdat

by the aforementioned subversive libertarian thinkers Ayn Rand, Friedrich Hayek, Count Chocula, and others. They spent money to build an intellectual and media infrastructure that would take their message to the people. By the early 1960s they were ready to unveil a new, vigorous conservatism to replace the stuffy, country-club Republicanism of years past: A bold defense of economic and personal liberty. A muscular military. Down with government meddling, from zoning regulations to taxes to civil rights laws.

These appeals found a ready audience, among not only the white Southerners who had been diaping out since *Brown v. Board of Education* but also the new generation of suburban strivers. These puds had grown fat and happy in the Keynesian hothouse of the 1950s and yearned for a freakier, more daring capitalism that would give them the status of true gods: a world where they would break the shackles of regulation, where merciless competition would see the best and strongest rewarded for their power, where Communism would be vanquished—not appeased—and where uppity minorities would truly learn their place again. An army of suburban warriors, fired up by this activist reactionaryism, stormed the GOP and nominated Arizona senator and human Lego Barry Goldwater for the presidency in 1964. But most voters at the time still believed that the media was an impartial arbiter of truth rather than a cultural Marxist brainwashing machine, so when the papers said Goldwater was a dangerous extremist, folks believed them. Goldwater got crushed, and liberals got the Great Society.

The Silent-but-Deadly Majority

Sicko libs didn't have too long to gloat, however. The 1960s saw the inherent and irreconcilable contradictions of liberal society explode into open conflict. The civil rights movement, the war in Vietnam, and a generalized youth culture revolt saw many more middle-class white people coming around to the Goldwaterite analysis of America: it had gone soft. It coddled criminal minorities and Communists here and abroad. The times demanded a return to hierarchy and control, and if that meant sabotaging the burgeoning welfare state, then so be it. Richard Nixon took this reactionary discontent and made it respectable and mainstream. No one could accuse old Dick Nixon of being a fringe crank like Goldwater. His command of the issues and connections to establishment conservatism were unsurpassed. Nixon rode a wave of disenchantment and media acquiescence to a narrow victory in 1968, but paradigm shifts take time. He had to deal with a Congress dominated by New Dealers and was forced to govern from the center-left on domestic policy.

But in the arena of culture, Nixon stoked social conflict and positioned himself as the tribune of the little guy, the silent majority, the hard hat who had been shouted down and bullied by agitating minorities and smart-mouthed student brats. The taciturn bigots helped Nixon roll to a historic blowout win over George "Acid, Amnesty, Abortion, Adult Baby" McGovern. Yet Nixon's project was undone by the Watergate scandal, in which he sent spies to bug Democratic National Committee headquarters in order to find out whether Jane Fonda liked him or, you know, *liked him* liked him, which gave the foundering Democrats a new grip on power.

Jimmy Carter came into office with Republicans fully discredited by Watergate and Democrats in control of both houses of Congress, just in time to oversee the dismantling of the New Deal policy consensus. Rising foreign competition to American industry, skyrocketing energy prices, galloping inflation, and cost overruns on NASA's *Six Million Dollar Man* project caused a crisis for capitalism in the 1970s. Rates of profit collapsed, and firms felt they could no longer afford the postwar deal they had made with workers for union recognition and high wages in exchange for labor peace. With the ruling class unwilling to budge on their monocle allowances, profits would have to be maintained at the expense of labor. So Carter carried out a policy of high interest rates and deregulation that helped the 1 percent get their libertarian revolution without even having to win any elections.

It's All for You, Jodie Foster

By the time Ronald Reagan successfully snared the Republican nomination for president in 1980, the stage was set for a politics of purely reactionary cultural grievance. Neoliberal reform of the economy had been implemented without much in the way of public debate or voter input. Reagan's campaign took this right-wing economic reality and ran with it, promising an unfettered capitalism that would work to reinstitute the hierarchical social relationships of pre-1960s America.

But a strange thing happened over the next few decades: the economy became markedly more savage and immiserating. Incomes stayed flat or declined as productivity rose and CEO pay exploded; deindustrialization obliterated entire swaths of the country; and stable middle-class jobs were replaced by precarious part-time service-industry ones. All the while, the cultural drift that had originally alienated and enraged white suburbanites in the sixties accelerated. The underlying racial order, codified by redlining and mass incarceration, remained largely undisturbed, but the flow of culture—from television and movie portrayals to news media framing—resisted control by grassroots reactionaries. For the most part, these right-wingers were people who had grown secure in the waning days of the New Deal consensus era and lived lives of comfort and ease. But even when you're master of the land, you rage at your inability to control the tides.

Slick Willie Style

After Reagan and his temporary replacement, George H. W., shuffled out of office, the 1990s dawned as a decade of indiscriminate dudgeon at an indiscreet presidency and culture. The Right hated Bill Clinton less for his policies (most of which were borrowed from the GOP, much as Nixon's were borrowed from his New Deal Congress) than for his status as an avatar of 1960s licentiousness. Pat Buchanan—the Hitler-sympathizing reactionary who held George H. W. Bush to 53 percent of the vote in the New Hampshire primary by railing against sodomy, Jewish pressure, women in the workplace, and African immigration*—gave the game away in his prime-time "Culture War" speech to the 1992 Republican National Convention:

* "I think God made all people good, but if we had to take a million immigrants in, say Zulus, next year, or Englishmen, and put them in Virginia, what group would be easier to assimilate and would cause less problems for the people of Virginia?" Pat Buchanan, quoted in E. J. Dionne Jr., "Is Buchanan Courting Bias?" *Washington Post*, February 29, 1992.

> This, my friends, is radical feminism. The agenda that Clinton and Clinton would impose on America—abortion on demand, a litmus test for the Supreme Court, homosexual rights, discrimination against religious schools, women in combat units—that's change, all right. But it is not the kind of change America needs. It is not the kind of change America wants. And it is not the kind of change we can abide in a nation that we still call God's country.

In the *28 Days Later* red-pupiled eyes of the Right, Clinton was a flag-burning, pot-smoking, USSR-visiting philanderer who, with his cookie-hating lawyer wife by his side, clambered over a heap of dead Arkansawyers to steal the White House with just 43 percent of the vote. One didn't have to be a sovereign citizen under the unfringed flag of Ruby Ridge to divine that Slick Willie was an illegitimate president. For all his Third Way–ism, Clinton *did* undo Reagan-Bush abortion restrictions, let closeted gays serve in the military, and sign an assault weapons bill that took everyone's dang guns away. With no major economic policy differences between Clintonite pragmatism and GOP orthodoxy (while the former at least accepted a social safety net, both supported NAFTA, the line-item veto, and prioritizing deficit reduction), culture-war issues and latent racial animus became more salient priorities to voters. After all, one party was promising to put an end to the daily baby Holocaust and throw Cadillac-driving welfare queens in prison, while the other was offering James Carville–garbled bromides about fiscal responsibility and "investing in opportunity." Team Clinton's feeble attempts to find middle ground with reactionary suburbanites—decrying black "superpredators" and Sister Souljah—proved unsuccessful in withstanding the electoral tidal wave propelled by the burgeoning populist right.

In 1994, Newt Gingrich inner-tubed that wave of resentment straight into the speaker's chair. Joining Newt's Republican Revolution were such solons as Bob Dornan, who had recently outed a gay colleague and told a reporter that "every lesbian spear-chucker in this country is hoping I get defeated,"* and Col. Ollie North, who had committed some light treason by selling weapons to Iran and raised over $20 million from direct-mail solicitations (an early form of Kickstarter) to GOP grassrooters in his losing Senate bid.

This new Republican Congress set about dismantling welfare, shutting down the government, and banning third-trimester abortions. But the antiestablishment fervor of right-wing voters—stoked by "feminazi"-hating outsiders like Rush Limbaugh, who was feted as the "Majority Maker" and made an honorary member of the class of '94—was hardly sated by Newt's modest changes to Congressional Process.

In 1996, Pat Buchanan was back, baby—this time wielding a literal pitchfork to continue his peasant revolt against Washington, DC, which he thought was once a nice Southern town "before all that crowd† came rolling in and took it over." Despite a brief stint as front-runner, Buchanan lost the nomination, yet the old-style racial resentment at the amorphous DC establishment articulated by his campaign continued to metastasize. Buchanan later abandoned the GOP, announcing, "Neither Beltway party is going to drain this swamp," but his brigades of aggrieved white suburbanites stayed,

---

* Francis X. Clines, "Appearing Nightly: Robert Dornan, Master of the Put-Down," *New York Times*, June 27, 1995.

† Black people.

placated for the time being by the siren song of "compassionate conservatism" and a glibly pious cowboy LARPer from Texas.

Bush Was Right

Based on the trajectory of his domestic agenda, George W. Bush was destined to be a one-term president. He inherited the dot-com bust, a recession, and a massive corporate-accounting scandal. His priorities were a tax cut for the rich and a bipartisan bill with Ted "Chappaquiddick" Kennedy to inject the feds into public education. Sure, the frothing populist base got some weak-sauce pandering with stem cells and faith-based bullshit, but with Clinton and his blow job crimes receding in the rearview mirror, the grand old coalition of big business and lunkheads seemed destined to fracture. If only there were some sort of banner or, perhaps, flag they could all rally around . . .

The 9/11 attacks finally gave the ambient cultural grievances of grassroots conservatism direction, focus, and energy. The global War on Terror became a fighting faith for the twenty-first century. This particular American combination of protestant wrath and militarized nationalism unleashed itself on the world, and woe betide any Arab or Frenchman who got in its way. The invasions of Iraq and Afghanistan were blood rituals, sacrifices to a God who embodied a pure, retro vision of America in which the cultural pollutants of feminism, secularism, and multiculturalism were purged with fire. And no petty class grievances could ever disunify the GOP base, so engaged were they in the holy quest that gave new meaning to their lives.

For an on-the-ground view of the populist right during the Bush years, here's a first-person report from our own Matt Christman:

Sometime after the invasion of Iraq, I worked in the bursar's office of a public university in the Midwest. I spent my days typing up labels for files and updating student information in an open bullpen. I was accompanied by a few sounds: the piped-in nursing-home music of the local smooth jazz station and, from the office behind me, the soft murmuring of local right-wing talk radio and the wrenching, wheezing cough of the man inside. His name was Neil, and he was a thin, balding man with glasses and a failing mustache. His job was to badger students who were delinquent on their loan payments; otherwise, he listened to local talk-radio shitheads and coughed.

One day I came into work and his office was empty. My boss told me that Neil was dead and that I should clean out his desk. There wasn't much in there besides a travel-sized cologne bottle and some hard candy. The only other personal touch in the office was an editorial cartoon that Neil had cut out and pinned to his corkboard, depicting Uncle Sam standing on the deck of an aircraft carrier next to a row of fighter jets. He said, "Can Saddam come out and play?" This man had spent the last years of his life slowly suffocating and being yelled at by broke college students, his only source of pleasure and purpose coming from his imagined connection to the violent triumphs of the American military.

Ever since then, I think of Neil whenever I contemplate the relentless militarized nightmare of the War on Terror. At the grassroots level, support for obscene military spending and imperial bloodletting satisfies a deep psychic need among neutered and demoralized American men.

I ate the dead man's candy and threw the rest of his shit out.

Jingoism, fear, and explicit homophobia propelled the Republicans to an electoral high-water mark in 2004 (as of this writing, the only time since the 1980s that they won the presidential popular vote). But despite the bodies piling up in Iraq and the yellow-ribbon magnets plating entire car bumpers, those ancient tensions—people vs. establishment, slobs vs. snobs, plucky poor-kid summer camp vs. posh rich-kid summer camp—began to rise from their slumber.

White suburban boomers were aging and getting ornerier, growing ever more concerned about the proximity of millennials to their lawn. Despite whatever liberalizing drugs they'd consumed in the 1960s, they were now being fed a steady diet of unadulterated rage from scaremongering local TV news, AM talk radio, Fox News, crypto-fascist publishing grifters, FreeRepublic.com, chain e-mails from Bill Cosby warning of the looming saggy-pants crisis, and the nascent right-wing blogosophere. It gave them a junkie's craving for something harder than Bill Frist or Roy Blunt.

And soon the slumbering wyrm revealed itself: Bush's clumsy second-term attempt to privatize Social Security may have pissed off the AARP, but what really raised the hackles of the GOP base was *shamnesty*: the bipartisan bill to beef up border security, revise guest-worker visas, and offer a grueling path to citizenship for undocumented immigrants. Not even such seasoned statesmen as Lindsey Graham and John McCain could sell a Kennedy-cosponsored bill to their apoplectic ward heelers, who drew a line in the desert over letting brown people become legal residents. The rancor spilled over into the 2008 primaries, in which the right wing viewed McCain with suspicion or hostility for the immigration bill and his bleeding-heart opposition to using medieval torture techniques on Muslims. To placate the grunts, he ran on generic "country first" militarism, highlighting all the villages he napalmed in Indochina to distract from the fact that this privileged son of an admiral wasn't exactly a CHUD himself. When that didn't cut it, he chose, in a desperate act with far-reaching consequences, to elevate one of their ranks to the ticket.

Sarah Palin, a certified brain genius who has read every newspaper, awakened a primal urge in the populist Right. She proved that one of their own could stand on the national stage spewing verbal diarrhea and, quite possibly (if not for the machinations of the biased lib media), end up a heartbeat away from the presidency. Not coincidentally, McCain's rallies in the home stretch devolved into screams of "Terrorist!" and "Liar!" and jeers at *their own candidate's* feeble calls for civility. One rally full of Minnesota-nice conservatives featured a man cryptically telling McCain, "Obama will lead the country to socialism! The time has come, and the Bible tells us: 'You speak the truth, and that the truth sets you free.' " Another woman told him, "I can't trust Obama. I have read about him, and he's not, he's not, uh—he's an Arab," to which McCain responded, Dear God, no, trust me, he's not an Arab, he's a normal person, I promise.*

---

* Jonathan Martin and Amie Parnes, "McCain: Obama Not an Arab, Crowd Boos," *Politico*, October, 10, 2008.

Dog Days of Obummer

Then the Gay Muslim Marxist Canine-Eater won. America, Reagan's shining city on the hill, vanished in a cloud of Choom smoke. Obama spent four years krumping on the Constitution, and real Americans had to just sit back and take it.

Take it they did, but not well. Almost as soon as Obama was inaugurated, the country's reserve population of cranks, gunfuckers, and Revolutionary War cosplayers strapped teabags to their tricorne hats and staged armed occupations of JCPenney parking lots from coast to coast. They watched Fox News with the reverent intensity of an astronomer witnessing the explosion of a supernova. They forwarded e-mails about secret mosques in the White House basement and Facebook memes demanding to see Obama's birth certificate. Such an awful and alien being simply could not be a real American. He had to have hatched from a glistening black egg in a sun-cursed Kenyan village, then slouched toward Washington, DC, in the dark of night. For the Right, the only psychic balm of those years was bearing witness to Obama's relentless parade of scandals, frauds, outrages, and humiliations, all of which ensured that he would go down in history as a Carteresque failure who would keep Democrats out of any national power for a generation.

Then he won again! Despite four years of craven appeasement and bowing and telepromptering and fifty-seven-states-ing and being from Kenya and *Fast and Furious* movies and LETTING OUR OPERATORS DIE AT BENGHAZI and lying about keeping my doctor and killing that fly and latte-saluting and putting his feet up and ACORN and Candy Crowley, dead and illegal voters somehow snuck that Muslim Brotherhood sleeper agent back into the White House no more White House more like Black House black as his heart blacker and blacker and blacker into the depths of hell where no light reaches lost in darkness forever the names of demons in the air rapped like a hip-hop barbecue tan suit tan as the skin of a lost and beaten ambassador bent at the knee sorry so sorry so so sorry for my evil white country logic and proportion fallen sloppy dead no more no more than Hillary witches sabbath out damned spot Vince Foster in moonlight no hope a lesser Bush milkwhite soul milkwhite blood please clap rhinoceros grazing in blank impotence what is this the sound of thunder the rumble of horse hooves the flowing blond mane buffeted by wind sword in hand shield in hand crimson billed crown atop his head fired, Obama FIRED HILLARY FIRED AMERICA MADE GREAT AGAIN the GLORIOUS WEALTH ORANGE SILKEN TRIUMPH GOLDEN VICTORY THE FINEST THE FINEST PERFECT LIPS PERFECT MOUTH SNEER OF COLD COMMAND APPRENTICE TO CHRIST COMMANDER OF RIGHTEOUSNESS LOCK HER UP FRENCH CANADIAN BEAN SOUP MICHIGAN WISCONSIN PENNSYLVANIA A ROSE PUSHING THROUGH CORPSES FAKE NEWS REAL NEWS REAL VICTORY REAL CLEANSING THE WALL THE WALL THE WALL OH MAMA OH MAMA PLEASE DON'T TEAR DON'T RIP JOBS JOBS JOBS YES I SAID YES I WILL MAGA MAGA MAGA ARE YOU TRIG-

GERED ARE YOU TRIGGERED ARE YOU TRIGGERED ARE YOU TRIGGERED ARE YOU TRIGGERED ARE YOU TRIGGERED ARE YOU TRIGGERED ARE YOU TRI-GGERED ARE YOU TRIGGERED ARE YOU TRIGGERED ARE YOU TRIGGERED ARE YOU TRIGGERED ARE YOU TRIGGERED ARE YOU TRIGGERED ARE YOU TRIGGERED ARE YOU TRI GGERED ARE YOU TRIGGERED ARE YOU TRIGGERED ARE YOU TRIGGERED ARE YOU TRIGGERED ARE YOU TRIG-GERED ARE YOU TRIGGERED ARE YOU TRIGGERED ARE YOU TRIGGERED ARE YOU TRIGGERED ARE YOU TRIGGERED ARE YOU TRIGGERED ARE YOU TRI-GGERED ARE YOU TRIGGERED ARE YOU TRIGGERED AM FEW A MOTHER'S BOY HAS NEVER WEPT NOR DASHED A THOU-SAND KIM CHIGGERED CARBPOO TIGGER BARGOOTROGERRRR

Schizopolis

Their brains broken by the cognitive dissonance of worshiping a country governed by someone who represented everything they fear and loathe, American right-wingers completely snapped and embraced the nihilistic spectacle of President Donald Trump. Much ink has since been dedicated to the question: Why? Here's a couple of drops: Because Trump does to liberals and minorities exactly what they thought Obama did to conservatives. Politics has become a realm of purely spiteful grievance. The only way out of this state of gibbering resentment is a positive vision, one that reconciles the concept of "America," which right-wingers hold sacred, and the fetid reality of multiculturalism and moral decay they see all around them. This vision is currently the one being promoted by the nascent white nationalist movement, which recognizes that the only way for America to conform to the glittering homeland they see in their heads is for the minorities and leftists and liberals and (((media types))) to be driven from the land. Only then, in a country re-founded on blood and soil, will the Starbucks barista write "Cool Dude" on your cup without rolling her eyes.

Remember—and remember well—that anyone who tries to feed you a line about how Donald Trump is not a "real" conservative is absolutely full of shit or is trying to sell you the next big lie. Trump represents everything that this vicious and corrupt project has valorized and promoted for the last forty years, and what's more, the disasters of right-wing governance have created a country exactly as stupid and desperate as the one that actually elected a buffoon like him. The problem Trump now presents for the conservative intelligentsia is that he's simply too much like the hogs who've been lapping up the slop of conservative ideology for decades and not enough like the undead ghouls who've been ladling it out. Since he has absolutely no intellectual foundation, he lacks initiation in the rites, rituals, and codes that have allowed previous conservatives to present themselves as thoughtful.

So strap in, folks. This is only the beginning. Trump himself, with his Heritage Foundation brain trust and Goldman Sachs cabinet, may look like a creampuff compared to the next generation of Republican demagogues who take the bloodthirsty, nativist, white-power ideology far more seriously.

Taxonomies

Bow-Tie Dipshit

You remember the kid who carried a briefcase to school since he was eleven? He grew up into this creature. A very specific subset of right-wing anti-intellectual intellectual, the Bow-Tie Dipshit represents the upper crust of the conservative movement. Loathed by his peers from college and beyond for reminding teachers that they've forgotten to assign homework and for reporting his roommate to the FBI for having sex, a robust hatred of academia nevertheless courses through every molecule of the Bow-Tie Dipshit's body. That body can currently be found enjoying lifetime tenure at Stanford's Hoover Institution or George Mason University's Mercatus Center.

Indeed, valorizing the pastimes and tastes of the conservative base is the main function of the Bow-Tie Dipshit. Where your average dipshit rube yelled "Shut up and play!" at the Dixie Chicks in 2003, the Bow-Tie Dipshit channeled his everyman populist rage into a three-thousand-word piece for his vanity project the *Clarion Criterion* about how the conductor of the New York Philharmonic attacked him personally by calling George W. Bush an "ignoramus." This results in endless books, articles, and quotes cribbed from Thucydides about why NASCAR, hunting, smoking cigarettes, driving a hundred-thousand-dollar pickup, eating hog fat, etc., is the culturally and philosophically correct pastime as opposed to the frivolous and elitist hobbies (drinking wine, drinking coffee, sodomy) of the coastal types that Bow-Tie Dipshit spends all his time around.

BACK CATALOG: *Sell Your Child and Save: A Guide to Austrian Economics*; *Baseball: The Most Beauteous Sport*; *Modern Pericles: Why George W. Bush Will Join the Pantheon of Classical Heroes*

FAVORITE COLORS: Periwinkle, mauve, chartreuse, seersucker

Euripides Theophanes
Aristophanes Ovid
Phrynichus Pericles
ROAD TO SERFDOM
AUSTRIAN

YouTube Logic Guy

This species is a hybrid synthesized from several preexisting ones. The Message Board Atheist, the Libertarian Logical Fallacy Man, and the Age of Consent Warrior all existed as separate entities in the earlier days of the Internet, times when different types of people were cordoned off in different webrings that unified like-minded peoples. But ever since the vast online worlds merged into a few main social networks, these previously distinct species began to interbreed, chiefly to take on the incursion of disruptive, illogical species into their shared space.

From their asexual reproductive methods emerged YouTube Logic Guy. Platforms like Facebook and Twitter were *somewhat* hospitable to this mutated progeny, but Twitter's character limits imposed ceilings on the level of genius he was allowed to dispense at one time, while Facebook's insistence on using real names prohibited the bravest soldiers of truth from employing all the weapons in their arsenal. It was not until YouTube was discovered that they could settle into an ecosystem that truly nurtured their biology, a platform that allowed them to stare directly into a webcam and talk about how *Miracle on 34th Street* misinforms children that it's okay to not use reason for three hours at a time.

While YouTube Logic Guy's deformities—such as unearned intellectualism and obsession with boring-ass books that suck shit—may confuse the untrained into thinking he's just an energy drink–swilling variant of the Bow-Tie Dipshit, he is vastly different. While the Bow-Tie Dipshit loves long-dead European authors, YouTube Logic Guy likes only one deado—Christopher Hitchens—and usually defers to living writers such as Sam Harris and GamemasterAnthony.

TOP VIDEOS ON YOUTUBE LOGIC GUY'S CHANNEL: Golden Retriever gets OWNED for Violating NAP; Monkey Bars, Kangaroo Court! My Unlawful Ejection from the Playground; LapBand Rants: Sarkeesian Destroyed; SJW Doctors Botch Logic Guy's Gastric Bypass RIP Tribute Video

FREE WILL
SAM HARRIS

Oligarch Monopoly Man

These are the guys who actually stand to benefit from all the atavistic racism, mindless resentment, and puerile spectacle commodified and propagated by the other people on this list. Every time an alt-right grifter Persicopes himself owning SJW college students or Fox News reports that the United Nations is using your tax dollars to breed a new type of SuperMuslim or your uncle ruins Thanksgiving dinner by shooting your biracial cousin with a crossbow, Oligarch Monopoly Man gets a percentage point knocked off his tax liability. He's a man of absurd wealth, likely gained through the hard work of his Nazi-collaborating father or slave-trading great-grandfather, and he wants to keep it. All of it. His plan for doing so involves sprinkling dark money over every perverse reactionary media project and politician he can find while he cosplays as a salt-of-the-earth cowboy who definitely knows how to ride a horse.

As America sinks further into mutual acrimony and paranoia, Oligarch Monopoly Man stacks that cash. Teen blood transfusions, cryochambers, and mech suits don't come cheap, and it costs a lot of money to build a perfect replica of the set of the Jean-Claude Van Damme film *Hard Target* to be stocked with the most dangerous game of all: man. But the most important reason it's worth destroying the earth to hold on to your precious lucre is as simple as it is expensive: immortality. Most Oligarch Monopoly Men achieve immortality the old-fashioned way: by leaving a vast financial empire to their half-wit children, who promptly contract syphilis and blow the whole fortune on prosthetic dicks.

IDEOLOGICAL NONCONFORMITY: Family built oil pipelines and infrastructure for Hitler *and* Stalin

PERCENTAGE OF AMERICA'S WEALTH CURRENTLY BEING HOARDED: 20 to 30

RIGHT-WING THINK TANKS AND MAGAZINES CURRENTLY FUNDING: All of them

WORLD WAR II
MEMORABILIA
CLAW!

Neocon Cuck

The first examples of these organisms showed up in their Ivy/sub-Ivy institutions as young Trotskyist tadpoles, their heads filled with the worst affectations of upper-middle-class intellectuals. But upon entering Leo Strauss's University of Chicago, each and every one mutated into a large, disgusting frog whose genetic purpose was to remake the world. These bowling-pin-shaped jackoffs matriculated into the departments of state and defense and declared themselves to be Russia experts as part of a Ford-era intelligence shop called Team Beta, which analyzed Russia and came up with reasons to arm what would eventually become Al Qaeda. After some mysterious violent group these guys had nothing to do with brought down the Twin Towers, these sons-of-CIA-funded-academics had a golden opportunity to utilize the nativist rage and bloodlust of bumpkins and middle-class authoritarians alike to kick off the virtuous wars the philosopher kings had wanted for years. The Neocon Cucks helped us dive dick first into Afghanistan and Iraq.

Trump was the best thing that ever could have happened to them. He lacks the veneer of propriety these sleazes need to remain friends with equally repellent liberal elites. As a result, many Neocon Cucks have been heralded as valorous, patriotic conservatives, welcomed into the #Resistance, and rewarded with cushy gigs as op-ed columnists in "respectable" liberal media outlets. It doesn't matter that they stoked the same racist impulses Trump did to get their wars. The fact that they want the same norms is enough for people.

GREATEST ASSET: Being the nephew of someone important

WORK HISTORY: Opening letters for Father, answering phones for Daddy, showing Papa how to use the computer, editing articles for the Old Man after dementia slows the old workhorse down, defending the Captain after his seminal piece "The Problem with Negroes" becomes public knowledge again, serving as editor in chief of *Commentary* and/or the *Weekly Standard*

Liberty Babe

She's conservative, she's traditional—and she's *hot*! *Awoooga!* It's Liberty Babe—a conservative media personality who appeals to an audience of mostly Social Security–age men hungry for books that reinforce their cosseted worldview and whose jackets give their lonely trouser worms a jolt of life. After her bestselling screeds *Betrayed, Mugged,* and *Defiled,* her latest release, *Gangbanged: How Weak RINOs and the Looney Left Are Spit-Roasting America,* is lighting up the Daily Caller comments section.

She's a lady, but she also watches football, drinks bourbon, and can field-dress a buck. She may not write her own books, but Liberty Babe will passionately defend their ideas against the limp-wristed liberal pajama boys Fox News keeps refrigerated in the greenroom. Also, sorry, haters: she doesn't have time for turncoat colleagues who've sullied the memory of Chairman Roger Ailes and accused him of depraved sexual abuse—she knows doing a twirl for a lecherous eighty-year-old hemophiliac while he bleeds through his pants is simply the price of entry into the boys' club. But just in case public sentiment does turn against the Fox conglomerate, she's got her own show—*Muzzle Flash*—on the NRA's digital-only channel. Each episode features her shooting a liberal in the back of the head and lighting his body on fire while the sprinkler system goes off, getting everyone's tops a little moist as Liberty Babe goes off on a viral pro-gun rant. She signs off by shooting another liberal in the head and making out with his widow.

CATCHPHRASES: "Gentlemen prefer guns," "Greenhouse gases get me hot"

UPCOMING BOOK: *Dirty Sanchez: The Left's Plan to Turn America Gay and Mexican*

Daughter Defender

It's no secret that the American institution of fatherhood is under attack from activist family-court judges, sex perverts, and ISIS-style immigrants. While most allow this institution to shrivel away like so many manhoods, there are a few brave vanguards in the American suburbs who act as Knights Templar to fellow dads. They prefer garish clothing replete with shiny angel wings and words like "LOYALTY," but their most holy garments are shirts that outline rules for dating their daughters. Yes, these men oppose foreign appeasement and gender tyranny, but their biggest fear is the sexuality of their baby girls. The Daughter Defender's every moment is spent fantasizing about a murky sicko (be they terrorist, Black Lives Matter thug, or boy in the wrong type of bucket hat) harming his daughter, allowing him to put his weekend martial arts training into practice. We can safely surmise that, for all the Daughter Defender's outward masculinity, this brick of unreleased rage and violence wishes he *were* his daughter.

Rules for Dating the Daughter

1. Get a job
2. Pull up your pants
3. Realize I'm watching you
4. You kiss her, I kiss you
5. Have her at my front door at 9:00, be in my toolshed at 9:30
6. Take pictures of your muscles and send them to me
7. Know that you are sexting both of us
8. Know that I'm a former high school wrestling coach
9. I don't mind going back to jail (for child pornography)
10. It may be her first time, but it's not mine

DONT TREAD O
POW★MIA
WANNA FUCK MY DAUGHTER?
GOTTA FUCK ME FIRST!

Citizen Kek

A few hundred years ago, the socially dislocated middle-class male could ship off to one of his nation's colonies and transform from virginal caterpillar to steely-eyed butterfly after successfully killing another man. With more and more fucked-up, isolated young men in the middle class but fewer colonies to send them to, the options for these people are dwindling. Sure, there's ISIS, but in the West, we have something else. No, it's not our military—the military is where you go if you really need a communications degree and you've accepted the risk of dying and killing for it. Besides, you have to run and spend time away from your computer. For those who are truly dissociated from modern life, there is the alt-right.

Citizen Kek is inspired by great heroes of Christendom like Charles Martel, Constantine, Christopher Nolan's Batman, and the Doom Marine. Like his ISIS equivalent, he's repulsed by the pluralism, sexuality, and alienation of modern life. However, unlike his heathen counterpart, his ideology is centered on "saving the West." His sworn enemies are, in total: Islam, the Left, liberals, cereal companies, the video-game industry, and women with short hair. Brought into the fold of neofascism through some combination of thwarted pickup artist ambition, being banned from a video-game forum, and Mom dating Steve again, Citizen Kek now loves doing *ironic* metacomedy about how the Holocaust was good because, to him, "the strong" exterminating useless, subhuman people is *extra* ironic. In addition to his extremely funny admiration for Hitler, Citizen Kek is obsessed with declining white birth rates in the West and finding a way he can fight back against this trend.

TOP ALT-RIGHT TWITTER HANDLES: NeoReactionary Grimace, HemorrhoidalSaxon, Reinhard Drydick

TOP ALT-RIGHT HASHTAGS: #DeusVult, #whitegenocide, #cuckmom, #muhallowance, #incelrebellion

TradCath Weirdo

A relatively new subset of religious hysteric, the TradCath Weirdo is a blazer-clad nebbish who imagines himself to be a craggy but lovable character in a Kingsley Amis or P. G. Wodehouse novel—and cosplays to match. The result is a lot of tweed jackets, pipes, and upsetting facial hair with none of the good humor or charm that usually accompanies them. It's normal for reactionaries to rage against the modern world, but it's not as commonplace to encounter the esoteric affectations and Pitchfork.com-like criticisms that the TradCath Weirdo will expound through Scotch Egg breath. Imagine a Wes Anderson character but with the cool New Order song accompanying their entrance replaced by a Gregorian chant they self-flagellate to for forty-five minutes after seeing a particularly raunchy 2 *Broke Girls* subway ad.

Unlike many of his brethren on the Right, the TradCath Weirdo will often seek to distinguish himself by correctly identifying the horrors of capitalism. Unfortunately, his prescriptions for these problems are to bring back Latin mass and purge skirts with above-the-knee hemlines from network TV. Instead of directing his ire toward financial capital or duplicitous public servants, his psychic energy churns with Lovecraftian disgust and horror at childless couples. In fact, the TradCath Weirdo is so obsessed with fecundity and nonprocreating marriages that he represents the only type of contemporary white person that actively hates dogs.

TWEE AFFECTATIONS: Walking stick, cane, shillelagh, sitting stick, sleeping staff, shower cane

TIGHTEST FIT: Blazer made entirely of elbow patches, sleeveless cardigan vest made of badger hair, quadruple-pleated trousers, Gucci flip-flops

OVER/UNDER ON TIME BEFORE NEXT RELIGIOUS CONVERSION EXPERIENCE: Six months

Mee-Maw and Pep-Pep

We hesitate to generalize our audience, much less all Americans, but this is literally your grandparents. They come from an era when people had the common decency to say "Sir," "Ma'am," and "Boy, that's not the water fountain you're supposed to use." Somewhere along the line, some member of your family fucked up and showed them how to use the computer. After that, Mee-Maw and Pep-Pep were no longer limited to Fox News's daytime hit *Skirts and Suits: Heartland Headlines*; they became privy to thousands of websites and chain e-mails, all racing through Pep-Pep's dementia to see which one implodes his brain before the light finally goes out. When you go to their house, Mee-Maw and Pep-Pep have copies of books like *Mosquerade: How Your Kids' Magnet School Became a Madrassa* by Liberty Babe Tresta Kranberry on their shelves. Their eyes seem to imply that they've already run through their brain's allotment of deathbed DMT.

Despite the fact that their spines are shaped like ampersands and every moment loosens their grasp on reality, Mee-Maw and Pep-Pep always vote. They vote more than anyone you've ever known. Wonder how we now have three hundred congresspeople who ran on ending the Muslim Brotherhood infiltration of Panera Bread? Look at Mee-Maw and Pep-Pep hobbling down to the polling place rain, sleet, or shine.

MOST RECENT FORWARDED CHAIN E-MAILS: "West Indian home-care nurse stealing from me!" "UN Agenda 21 Seizing Rascal Scooters," "Bill Cosby Tells It Like It Is!" "Bible Code Revealed: Winning Bingo Numbers"

LAST CONSCIOUS THOUGHTS BEFORE DEATH: When will my Sean Hannity commemorative coins arrive?

GOLDLINE CERTIFIED™
FOX NEWS
MEASURING THE AFRICAN SKULL
NO SHANIA LAW

Actual Vampire

Right-wingers continue to lionize decades and even centuries past—but how many of them actually lived through those times?

The conservative movement is filled with boys who look like old men and old men who look like condoms packed with oatmeal, but astride them all are a proud few creatures of the night who technically died before the Reformation but show no signs of wear and tear. Legend has it that vampires first appeared in early-fifteenth-century Romania when a nobleman investigating Turkish "no-go zones" in the countryside attempted to use alchemy in order to protect himself from knockout gangs loyal to Mehmed I. Unfortunately for him (but fortunately for all lovers of debate and intellect), the nobleman was transformed into a horrible creature that could never die. This impossibly old and wicked monster came from a time before safe spaces and will probably use his hypnotic powers to get you to kill a family member, as that's the only kind of thing that entertains him anymore.

The Actual Vampire is so committed to old-fashioned manners that he will not enter a domicile unless he is specifically invited. While his clothing choices—mostly capes and cassocks—reveal a traditional sensibility, he is committed to the cool, urbane nightlife activities typical of an intellectual conservative. These bon vivants are known to levitate caddishly outside the windows of young men and women and hold rousing debates on the death tax. While they're usually considered to be of Eastern European origin, Actual Vampires now make their homes in the subbasements of brainy conservative institutions like the *National Review* and the Heritage Foundation.

SPECIAL ABILITIES: Can transform into a bat, casts no reflection in mirrors, immortality

WEAKNESSES: Sunlight, garlic, crucifixes, holy water, wooden stake through the heart, housing court judge

Can **YOU** help guide Michael Flynn and Michael Junior to capture the traitor **Gülen?**

Spot the **differences** between these images!

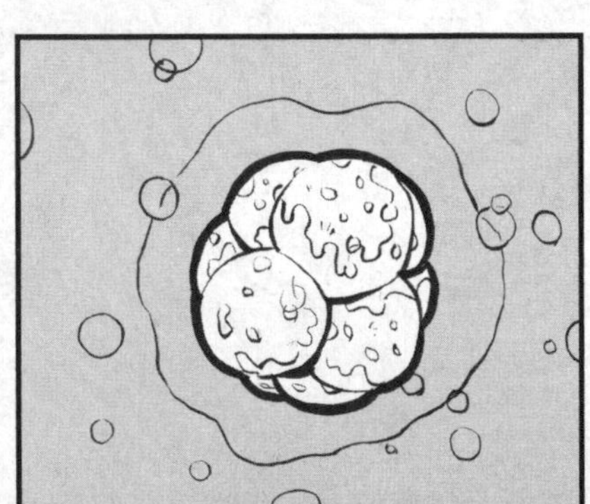

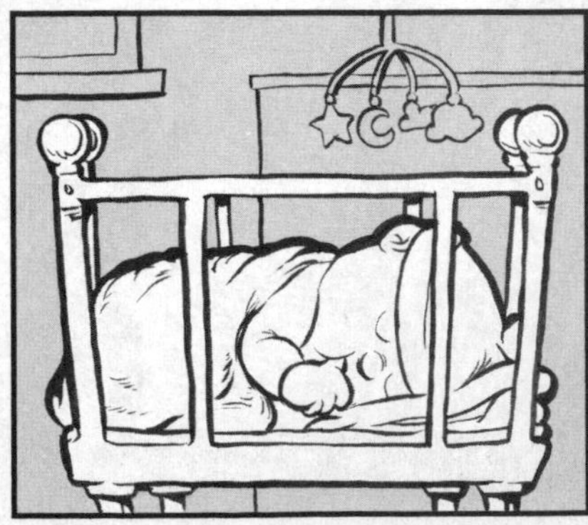

Find all the hidden words!

X Q S A F C O M E T E Y
A B R A M O V I C H Y V
M F J E Q P I H P D W Y
A Q O D S E W O I M P S
T E J C P P Z T N O O G
B E C I I P D D G T D V
⊦ Z G W R E I O P V E M
O P W Z I R A G O H S P
U I C Y T O W S N R T N
V Z K B J N E U G S A J
K Z R Z N I S T O R E C
H A N D K E R C H I E F

Connect the dots to see what **Daddy Trump** will do to the **Deep State!**

SPOT-THE-DIFFERENCE SOLUTION

There is no difference between the images. This section was sponsored by Operation Rescue.

CHAPTER FOUR

MEDIA

Take away the newspaper—and this country of ours would become a scene of chaos. Without daily assurance of the exact facts—so far as we are able to know and publish them—the public imagination would run riot. Ten days without the daily newspaper and the strong pressure of worry and fear would throw the people of this country into mob hysteria—feeding upon rumors, alarms, terrified by bugbears and illusions. We have become the watchmen of the night and of a troubled day.

—Harry Chandler

RIP my menchies.

—@Vox_Michael

xtry extry! Read all about it! "Daring Dirtbags Disrupt Daffy Democrats' Discombobulated Discourse!"

That's how this chapter might have read if we still lived in the ink-stained era of print news. Today, however, virtually all Americans get their news, opinions, and pornography through the Internet. How did we get from dead logs to live blogs, from editorial boards to circuit boards? Put on your newsboy cap and read on, because Chapo Trap House has the "scoop"!

Sir, Have You No Shame, Sir: A History of Journalism

The first mass-produced newspapers emerged in Germany shortly after the invention of the printing press. They included *Relation aller Fürnemmen und gedenckwürdigen Historien* (*Account of All Distinguished and Commemorable News*) and *Liste der bekannten Juden* (*List of Known Jews*). These publications disseminated vital information about current affairs to the literate masses.

The concept spread to London, where gazetteers on Fleet Street added such innovations as editorials and the Page 3 Slags. Across the Atlantic, a media culture flourished in the thirteen colonies, where the issues of the day were hotly debated within the pages of newsletters and pamphlets. Among the early commentators was a young publisher's apprentice named Benjamin Franklin. He was a polymath and the first true American man of letters, in that he generated reams and reams of extremely horny correspondence. As a sexual degenerate who disseminated totally useless advice to the ignorant masses (sample aphorism: "The fool wakes up to the cuckoo's crow whilst the wise man rises to the songbird of Reason"), Ben Franklin was also our nation's first pundit.

Out of the colonists' pamphleteering culture emerged an uncompromising devotion to freedom of speech, which produced such widely read radical polemics as *Common Sense* and *No Taxation Without Fringeless Flags*. After the Revolution, ratification of the proposed US Constitution was hotly debated through competing serials such as the *Federalist Papers* and the vastly more popular *Wow. I Had No Idea About These 10 Bills of Rights (Number 6 Will Shock You)*.

American journalism in the first part of the nineteenth century consisted mostly of libelous attacks on politicians' illegitimate octoroon children, classified ads for bounties on escaped slaves, and advice columns. Newspapers tended to be partisan outlets, loyal to single-issue parties like the Anti-Masonics and the Hose Down the Irish League. Some periodicals, however, were brave enough to challenge entrenched power. Notable among them was *Harper's Weekly,* which ran Thomas Nast's political cartoons depicting corrupt politicians as rotund gluttons with dollar-sign-adorned bags for heads (part of American media's long and disgraceful legacy of body-shaming) and showing the Catholic clergy as vicious crocodiles crawling out of the Potomac to hunt for children (part of the American media's long and honorable tradition of truth-telling). But such publications were few and far between.

Dearest Prudence: Letters Home from the Front

During the Civil War, newspapers were the primary means for the public to keep track of battles, campaigns, and how many cousins, nephews, and sons they had left. On assignment from big-city papers and news bureaus, Northern reporters embedded with the Army of the Potomac fed the public's inexhaustible appetite for war reporting and straight talk directly from the men in charge with exclamation-point-laden stories like "Friends Till the End! Lincoln and McClellan Pledge Loyalty to Each Other as the Winning Team the Union Needs!"

In addition to reporting the news, war correspondents also related common soldiers' day-to-day experiences amid the carnage and provided a conduit for them to share their firsthand accounts of the war. Many newspapers published soldiers' personal letters and diaries, often penned before major battles. Such missives gave a human face to the rank-and-file participants of this brutal conflict. They are also among the earliest known examples of the modern genre of the advice column, as many of these letters were sent directly to papers by soldiers seeking help with personal matters. Reproduced below is an example of one of these historical documents, originally published on July 17, 1862, by the *New York Daily Crier*.

My Dearest Prudence,

I am still among the living, though have taken ill and have decided to use my time in the diarrhea tent to compose a few lines to you on an issue that has vexed me much during these long months away from home. I have been married two and half score years to my beloved, whom we shall call Annabelle. She is the kindest, most beautiful object of my most assiduous affections. She is a wonderful mother to our—at last count—eleven children, and has been such a friend and companion to me that I dare not imagine a better or more divine specimen of the female species.

However, there is but one small problem that haunts our otherwise blissful wedded harmony. I speak of her excessive and often cruel condemnations of my mother's hardtack. I was raised eating mother's delicious dry biscuits with extra flour, and I fear Annabelle has always harbored a deep resentment of my Olympian regard for Mother's biscuits. This has boiled over as of late when, in my last correspondence, Mother mentioned she had given Annabelle a batch of her hardtack to send to me. However, when the package from home arrived, the hardtack was nary to be found, replaced by Annabelle's pickled onions. Should I confront Annabelle over her pilfering of my tack and risk having this be her last memory of me, or should I let this hound continue to sun itself on the porch in the late summer afternoon? Sometimes I fear that this cursed war and the problems betwixt Annabelle and my mother will never end.

Sincerely,

Aggrieved in Antietam

In the late Gilded Era a new model emerged, one in which the news could be underwritten by paid ads for Dr. Consham's Miracle Woman-Hysteria-Curing Tonic and opium-based baby formulas. Media magnates like William Randolph Hearst and Joseph Pulitzer snatched up local papers and forged the first news conglomerates. Political content slowly sank off their pages, replaced by lurid true-crime stories about debauched women exposing their bare shoulders on the beach, crotchety opinion columns about how Pullman porters weren't entitled to exorbitant half-penny tips, and, for illiterate consumers, comic strips.

It was also around this time that a Hearst paper led the country into war with Spain on false pretenses through breathless and selective reporting about the sinking of the USS *Maine* in Havana, a naval accident that was spun as evidence of Spanish aggression against America.

At a penny per copy, papers publishing such sensationalistic "yellow journalism" sold extremely well. But some readers craved more than just bulletins about Italian-on-Italian crimes and daily reports of President Taft's expanding waistline. Yellow papers could also be serious as well, as several Hearst titles published accounts of Bella Allabonne, a seven-year-old trapped in war-torn Belgium who urged President Wilson to "do something."

The Progressive movement spawned a class of hard-nosed investigative journalists who dedicated their lives to rooting out corruption, challenging the entrenched power of monopolists, exposing the horrifying conditions in which the working classes lived, and doing their best to make sure those working classes didn't breed too prodigiously. Fearless muckrakers like Upton

Sinclair, Ida Tarbell, and Jacob Riis showed how dedicated journalists could improve the lives of the millions by doggedly pursuing the truth.

But most journalists were not fearless muckrakers. Ninety-nine percent of newshawks were what we like to call "hacks."

In this era, long before Columbia J-School and valuable résumé-building unpaid internships, the job of reporting the news was not the province of failsons of the educated upper class like it is today. Instead, most journalists were the children of impoverished immigrants. They were the seventh sons of a proletariat deemed too sickly and weak to pursue a respectable child-labor trade like coal runner or Triangle Shirtwaister. These young cowards were plucked from the slums at an early age and sold to the Hearst Corporation.

The media industry put these amorphous lumps of raw humanity through a brutal baptism by fire. The cubs were instilled with a healthy fear of challenging entrenched power, taught to fairly report on both sides of any given issue—such as women's suffrage or lynching—and totally sequestered from contact with females so they would emerge from their chrysalides as weird sexual neurotics. The ones who survived earned the right to call themselves bona fide journalists.

Some of them became investigative reporters, adopting the moniker "gumshoe," a reference to their habit of stopping women on the street and offering to inspect their feet for grime, often even going so far as to offer a thorough tongue-cleaning, free of charge.

The cream of the crop became pundits—regular columnists

paid to pontificate about every single issue, with special emphasis on the issues they knew absolutely nothing about. In the rapidly modernizing world of the 1920s, when women's skirts were getting shorter and wearable tech like polio braces proliferated, the common man relied on these noble perverts to analyze, predict, and explain. To today's reader, the concept of an individual possessing a perfectly average level of intelligence and education (at best) shitting out half-baked analyses of complex political and social matters to be closely read by millions as if they were the divinely inspired words of a prophet descending a mountaintop may seem absurd. But remember that people were stupid back then and didn't have Yahoo! Answers and r/legaladvice to explain things to them.

Some examples of punditry from the early twentieth century:

- "Union Organizers Are Murdered in Some Parts of the Country, and That's Okay"
- "Why We Need a Second Great War to Toughen Up the Entitled 'Greatest' Generation"
- "What My Rickshaw Driver Taught Me about Nanking, the Next Up-and-Coming Global Hotspot"
- "Limiting the Workweek to Just 80 Hours Will Hurt the People It's Meant to Help"
- "Spanish Flu or Spanish Boo-Hoo? New Influenza Nothing to Worry About"

- "We Need to Talk about Al Jolson. Is He Ashamed of Being White?"
- "Civility and Compromise: Why the Weimar Republic Will Last for a Thousand Years"

No matter their specialty, these journalists all shared in the belief that their high salaries (seventy-three cents per annum) and total subservience to robber barons made them superior to normal human beings. They knew that their obvious physical and social deficiencies were more than compensated for by the strength of their minds, and that any criticism leveled at them was wholly due to the fact that others were just jealous and intimidated by their massive intelligence. Occasionally one of them would be publicly humiliated by the leaking of their private telegrams to Ida B. Wells, but overall, print scribes were the undisputed alpha males of the media.

Or so it was until the print guys were hit by a wave—a radio wave, to be exact. In the 1920s and '30s, radio (or "talkies") emerged as a news medium that could transmit live coverage of sporting events, political rallies, and Hindenburg explosions. With the advent of radio came a new form of slick demagoguery, exemplified by the most popular radio host of the Depression era, fascist anti-Semite Father Charles Coughlin.

Excerpt from a Transcript of The People's Pulpit *Radio Broadcast, August 5, 1938*

FATHER CHARLES COUGHLIN: Imagine my surprise when the conspiratorial Hebrew showed himself not just to be a wandering interloper of national affairs, not simply a cancer in our body, but painfully and proudly illogical. Time and time again, I have challenged "comedian" Jack Benny to debate me about his obfuscation about the factual claims I am making. When pressed to prove his claims that Jews are not infecting Caucasian Americans with buggery using pies and seltzer made with dark Talmudic science, he told me to "Take a hike into the lake, pal." This is the supposedly peaceful and easygoing Yiddish liberalism the media tells us about? Let's look at the facts: If I were to walk into a lake, I would most likely perish. When I simply ask him if he is using scientifically altered food to make Catholic fathers abandon their families for bathhouses, he issues a death threat. Furthermore, Sid Caesar has yet to condemn this political violence. Tell me this: If they truly believed in the merits of their arguments, why would they avoid a spirited debate?

As if there weren't enough war waged on Christian men by the psychotic liberal entertainment industry, *The Three Stooges Meet the Mummy* continues these Jewish-controlled attacks. Tell me, if these are just "comedy talkies," as abusive Bolshevik liberals insist to me they are in their many letters, why do all three of the Stooges get their feet caught in buckets in this production, thus revealing their location to the clearly Jewish mummy? Why have we seen similar such buffoonery in their previous entries, such as *The Three Stooges Meet Frankenstein* and *Dopes at Sea*, wherein their antics defy reason and show them repeatedly humiliated by several varieties of Draculas, Wolfmen, and Negroes? Yet when they encounter other whites such as wealthy dowagers, they attack them with pies. Explain to me how this makes logical sense, that these men would get the better of intelligent Caucasoids but are humiliated by Hebrew-like creatures. You cannot make such a good-faith argument. The "Stooges" are simply that—stooges for the Hollywood Jews who seek to emasculate Christian men by portraying them as mute,

dumb, and lame nincompoops who cannot paint a house or even move a heavy safe without saying "humina humina!"

That about does it for today. As always, please share this broadcast with your friends by inviting them over to listen to your radio. 'Bye, guys.

The outbreak of the Second World War gave radio the opportunity to prove it could be used for more than just broadcasting fascist propaganda. Radio correspondents stationed in Europe brought the war right into Americans' living rooms. A young CBS man named Edward R. Murrow issued gripping dispatches from the Blitz, each one heralded by his signature line, "This is London, brought to you by Stevenson & Sons Goiter-Be-Gone: When you absolutely, positively need your goiter gone before prom night, look for the Stevenson & Sons label."

After the war, television slowly grew to replace radio as the dominant news medium. Richard Nixon used it to defend his sending his adopted dog, Lamby, back to the shelter. Joe McCarthy used it to broadcast a list of known queers in the State Department, carefully compiled by his cool bachelor friend Roy Cohn. And a handful of brave journalists used it to push back against the preferred narrative of the ruling class. Among them were Martha Rountree of *Meet the Press*, Huntley and Brinkley of the *Huntley-Brinkley Report*, and Spy and Spy of *Mad Magazine Roundtable*. In 1954, addressing a soda jerk in the Annapolis, Maryland, malt shop where he had just been denied a third free refill on his root beer float, Edward Murrow coined the journalist's creed that would ring through the ages: "Have you no sense of decency, sir?"

It was also around this time that the media led the country into war with Vietnam on false pretenses through breathless and selective reporting about the government's version of the Gulf of Tonkin incident, a total fabrication that was used as evidence the North Vietnamese had attacked the United States.

Television brought Mr. and Mrs. Middle Class face-to-face with the bedlam of the 1960s: civil rights marchers mauled by dogs, protesters brutalized by Mayor Daley's thugs outside the 1968 Democratic National Convention, and the seemingly endless torrent of visceral carnage that spewed from Vietnam. As the nation's folk-poet laureate, Bob Dylan, put it, "Blood on the screen, Mr. Clean, can't wipe the sheen, with your dope fiend [harmonica solo]."

The terror in Indochina—massacres of innocents, soldiers fragging their commanding officers, endless exports of flag-draped coffins, and torturous comedy radio broadcasts by Robin Williams—gnawed at our nation's conscience. In an appearance on the *Smothers Brothers Comedy Hour*, Davy Jones famously declared, "This war's a bummer, huh. It's far out." Back in Washington, Johnson reputedly said, "If I've lost the Monkees, I've lost Middle America."

Meanwhile, in the print media, a different kind of revolution was taking place. At the top of the decade, novelist Theodore White took political reporting to a new level with his behind-the-scenes account of the 1960 election, *The Making of the President 1960*. Before White, campaign reporters were essentially stenographers, filing dry and matter-of-fact dispatches from the trail (e.g., "Whistle-stop at Akron, Ohio. A waterfowl gets itself embedded in the crevice between Mr. Taft's hefty bosom and generous gut whilst the candidate was in the middle of a hearty stemwinder against the Polack, much to the amusement of all but the be-periled Ohio Gentleman")

That all changed when White's gripping narrative, written in a novelistic style replete with psychological probing of powerful men and careful attention to symbol and conflict, showed that political reporting could be something more contextual and profound than transcription. Namely, it could be about the winners and losers of the week. It could be about which candidates have the "It" factor and which are failing to project strength and vision. About what the candidates' wives are wearing.

Since White, this new mode of nuanced, analytical political reporting—modulated by the insights of gimlet-eyed pundits—has helped guide voters to the 100 percent correct decision in every single presidential election. Reporters were further freed from the shackles of objectivity by the innovation of New Journalism, ushered in by Tom Wolfe's landmark *Esquire* article, "Encomium for the Whisky Slum High-Octane Junkie Rat Mothers *Kill Kill*!" about the Boy Scout Jamboree. And the drug-laced gonzo reporting of *Rolling Stone*'s Hunter S. Thompson further allowed egg-shaped pundits with nascent alcohol problems to think of themselves as outlaw rebels.

But journalists didn't truly reach the apex of esteem until two lowly print reporters brought down a president in their hit investigative series, *All the President's Men*.

Dustin Hoffman and Robert Redford were just two green reporters working for the legendary *Washington Post*. Redford's reporting style was classically handsome in a blond, all-American way, while Hoffman's writing was offbeat, shaggier, but no less dreamy. These two young guns combined forces to break one of the biggest stories of all time. Along with their memorable editor, the legendary Jason Robards, Hoffman and Redford beat the streets and worked the phones, turning what started out as a minor break-in at the Democratic Party's national headquarters into a conspiracy that went all the way to the White House. The reporting in *All the President's Men* is a popcorn classic that still holds up to this day.

With the reputation of the federal government and the military shattered after Watergate and Vietnam, journalism emerged as the most respected institution in the country. In the public imagination—and in their own—reporters and pundits were finally perceived as whisky-slugging alpha dogs, fearlessly challenging the powers that be, beating up sources in dark alleyways, and bedding woman after woman. By the end of the 1970s, they could carry themselves as thought leaders, opinion makers, and sex symbols. In children's bedrooms across the country, posters of Gerald Ford, Gen. Westmoreland, and Lt. Calley came down, to be replaced by cheesecake pinups of Rowland Evans and Robert Novak.

Journalists spent the coke-fueled 1980s living the dream. The nascent twenty-four-seven cable news channel CNN put frowzy pundits in front of cameras, increasing their celebrity and vanity. Meanwhile, America elected a Hollywood actor president, and unflinching, heroic newsmen got to the bottom of Iran-Contra, the S&L crisis, and AIDS denialism by demanding that Reagan tell them folksy stories about being friends with Tip O'Neill.

It was also just a little later that the media led the country into a war with Iraq on false pretenses through breathless and selective reporting on Saddam's regime, claiming it dumped Kuwaiti babies out of incubators—a total fabrication that was used as evidence the Iraqis were committing grotesque war crimes against an American ally.

The Gulf War and the O. J. Simpson trial, two high-budget TV specials produced by CNN, generated massive ratings for cable news, encouraging the establishment of imitators like MSNBC and Fox News. Conservative talk radio gave voice to the millions of reactionary white men who couldn't speak for themselves due to their mouths being stuffed with hoagies. The good ol' print world boomed as well, with innovative new magazines springing up, such as *George,* founded by John F. Kennedy Jr., and *Brill's Content,* founded by Steven Brill and sadly shuttered in 2001 for being too successful. Over in the UK, so-called lad mags like *Council Bottoms, Fanny Mates,* and *Rude* exploded in popularity. Even photojournalists got into the action by murdering Princess Diana.

Events like the Oklahoma City bombing, the Columbine massacre, and the White House–Lewinsky drama whetted the public's appetite for more stories, more gossip, more context, and more baseless speculation. Ad revenue was through the roof. The *New York Times* commissioned an $850 million skyscraper in Midtown Manhattan. In the words of *Times* publisher Arthur Ochs Sulzberger Jr., "The good times for newspapers will never, ever end."

Journalists were in high demand, commanding bigger and bigger salaries with less and less editorial oversight. A reporter with three months of experience could get $1 per word for transcribing a State Department press release (headline: "All's Well That Ends Well in Kosovo") and still make it to the bar by noon. Best of all, there was absolutely, positively no way for average people to talk back to journalists and pundits, to publicly call out hacks for their career failures and physical deficiencies, or to publish journalists' private correspondences with women twenty years their junior replete with winky faces and ambiguous complaints about their wife.

But that was all about to change.

Digital Media: Truth Gets an Upgrade

Throughout the 1990s, the Internet was a slumbering giant. Newspapers and publishers expected it to remain an alternative platform that mainly catered to Neopets enthusiasts and lovers of age-regression porn. In a 1998 column, *New York Times* elder wonk Paul Krugman summed up this frame of mind with his pedantic, antisocial flair:

> The growth of the Internet will slow drastically, as the flaw in "Metcalfe's law"—which states that the number of potential connections in a network is proportional to the square of the number of participants—becomes apparent: most people have nothing to say to each other! By 2005 or so, it will become clear that the Internet's impact on the economy has been no greater than the fax machine's.*

* Krugman's column, disappeared from the regular Internet, can still be found here: http://web.archive.org/web/19980610100009/www.redherring.com/mag/issue55/economics.html.

Unfortunately, a different law of the market, "Benzino's Paradox," ended up proving that people have a lot more to say to one another than Krugman assumed. Things like, "My personal review of *Halo 4*: Too Many Black Aliens," and "r u horni? cool!" This is the online landscape we have come to know, love, and take for granted. But back in the 1990s, before social media and shitposting, everyone running the newspaper and TV industries thought like Krugman. There was no real preparation for a massive shift in technology that would destabilize and ultimately destroy the print media's business model and leave them selling themselves even harder than they did in the old days when they hawked reverse mortgages and Doctor Haines' Golden Specific.

Instead, newspapers patted the newborn Internet on the head and gave it some of their print material to post online for free (including Krugman's dumbass column above). They planned to make money off it, of course, but the industry saw the Web as a sort of bonus market, a medium where distribution would be free, unlike the expensive chain of materials that delivered papers to homes and newsstands across the country through a complex series of News Tubes. Paying for that distribution was part of why they always needed big bucks from advertisers like Rolex, Blackwater, and the Church of Scientology.

But our media overlords made the classic mistake of feeding a Gremlin after midnight: in a flash, the Internet mutated from a cuddly novelty into a grotesque monster that gored its masters to death in a way that was alternately scary and entertaining.

These companies started to panic when readers understandably decided to get more and more of their news from the *free* Internet rather than paying for subscriptions. And so began the death spiral:

newspapers underestimated the Internet, posted their shit for free, then realized they would go broke unless they started charging for it. Problem was, readers had already tasted free and didn't feel like suddenly shelling out for Gerald Fletch-Queefen's latest column in the *Wall Street Journal*.

Blindsided, papers tried to make money off their new cyber-readers by running ads on the Internet the same way they did in print: banner ads, sidebar ads, and pop-ups, like the one you closed five minutes ago that tried to sell you fair-trade lube or the next generation of "Vapes for Latinos." This gave birth to the metric of Web traffic, the numbers that would be waved in front of advertisers as the new (and false) analog for print-circulation numbers. After ad-blockers fucked up that plan, too, publishers set up paywalls. Foiled again! A new breed of sites with ridiculous names like *Feed-Bag*, *NewsBoner*, and *Business Insider* cropped up, supplying aggregated* stories from other† sources, gratis. Pretty soon the Web's free real estate wasn't so free anymore, and, watching their print and digital ad revenue shrivel like a chilly scrotum, everyone from the *New York Times* to the *Mormon Science Sentinel* scrambled to build from scratch an entirely new edifice of *digital* media production, sales, and distribution.

Ever since then, a galaxy of news sites has exploded across the Internet: you have your *BuzzFeed* types, whose output is mostly memes stolen from Reddit, plus the occasional news article deciding whether the latest massacre in Syria is EPICWIN or LOLFAIL;

---

* Stolen.

† Original.

your *Politico* types, which take the bullshit, "objective" tone of legacy media and ratchet it up 200 percent for an even more elite market of scum-sucking DC consultants; and your more "partisan" news shops, like the *Huffington Post* on the yuppie-left and the *Federalist* on the Francoist-right, who reliably distribute pellets of nourishing, ideologically agreeable information to their respective audiences. These media creatures were native to the Web Zone. To quote Christopher Nolan's twisted philosopher Bane, the *Washington Post* merely adopted the darkness—*Vox* was born in it, molded by it.

Still, that hasn't given the moguls of News 2.0 any better ideas for a business model. Eventually, they *will* stop receiving truckloads of venture-capital money just for appearing "innovative" or "having a presence" and they'll be locked on the same ice floe as the old-timers. Everyone is fucked, with the exception of billionaire-backed sugar-daddy projects like *Bloomberg*, which exists because an insane elf manlet is willing to spend millions so he can see his name printed in a news outlet that *isn't* calling for his banishment from public life.

In the interest of helping any young oafs make a two-year career for themselves before all this blows up, we introduce to you here a guide to success in New Media.

How to Win Fake Friends and Influence Nobody

Journalism isn't the stuffy career path it used to be: instead of covering a beat at your local paper, working your way up the totem pole to a national outlet, and enjoying comfy union benefits all the while, the contemporary journalist can now embrace the life of the common deer tick, jumping from host to host until being plucked off and left to die in a pile of shit.

Indeed, most young reporters observe their local papers foundering and look to start their careers at one of the many hip, VC-backed news sites online—hell, you're a millennial, you know their names: *Mic, Vox, Vice, HuffPo, BuzzFeed, Dang-That's-News,* r/creepshots, *Sproing,* and *Fappe.*

The market is volatile, yes, but that doesn't mean you can't game the system with some lifehacks. Here are the steps anyone can follow to become part of the perpetually insecure floating labor reserve army of Digi-News.

1. **A Good Twitter Avatar:** People need to know that you're a legitimate journalist whose opinions on Russia can be taken seriously. For your avatar, use a screenshot of the one time you were on TV talking to a congressman's dumbest child about how the 2018 midterms are like *Jumanji.* If you've never been on TV, take a perfectly centered selfie from your chest up in which you have a smirking-yet-serious look on your face that says, "Sorry, we only serve facts here. But you can also get snark if you really want it."

2. **A Good Twitter Bio:** As a media kid, you'll need to signal-boost a lot of different news content, which will probably include some nasty right-wing cranks and racist bloggers. In your bio, warn your followers that retweets of these assholes *aren't* endorsements, even though they will almost certainly

end up as your colleagues and drinking buddies. If you're under thirty-five, include a fake job title like "Anti-cronut Activist" or "Honorary Canadian"; if you're over thirty-five, quote some turgid classic rock song with lyrics like, "Caught between left and right / Lookin' for truth in this fallen world."

3. **Good Tweets:** Don't share too many spicy political opinions, for which you could get disciplined or fired. Instead, quote-tweet everything, adding only "This x100!" or "Big if true." This is funny because the story is usually not true. Or, say something about the weather and then just write "Sad!" as Donald Trump would. This is funny because the user in question is someone other than Donald Trump. Keep eighteen-month-old puns and jokettes going—they'll *never* get stale.

4. **Good Tweet-ups:** Now you've hit the big time. Thanks to trenchant observations like "Hmm, fake news much?" you've achieved a level of notoriety sufficient to earn you an invite to a bona fide Journalism Happy Hour. Hop onto the surface train down to one of the worst bars New York or DC has to offer; some kind of always crowded watering hole for dead-eyed people called the Lanyard Lounge or Capitol Cloak Room where you'll get to meet the doughy whites behind the avatars. Regale the crowd with the latest memes and hot takes that everyone already knows because you're all chained to the same stupid website, get a little too tipsy on $7 Amstels, and find yourself in a handicap stall desperately making out with a thirty-seven-year-old *Medium* writer who's thinking about pivoting to improv comedy. You've earned it, rookie.

5. **Good Journalism:** Find some time to do this. Maybe post a C-SPAN video of a politician saying something different than what they're saying now. That's called an *exposé,* and it's the highest form of journalism.

So much for the exciting new world of digital media, an industry that in 2018 appears vast and thriving but is actually financially dependent on getting enough people to click on links like "One Weird Trick for Putting Your Dong in a Light Socket." With adblockers torpedoing the last scraps of traditional revenue, most news outlets are set to march into the twenty-first century as proud slaves to megacorporations like Facebook and Google, the last beacons of hope to get people to read anything.

The Shilling, or How I Learned to Stop Worrying and Love the Blog

Here we should pause to discuss a significant moment in the early 2000s, after the legacy media began to fail but before the new media kids like *BuzzFeed* and *Vice* took over. It's remembered as an exciting turn in the history of journalism—by the main character in *Memento*. In the real world, it produced some of the shittiest characters and methods of contemporary media.

We refer, of course, to the birth of the blogosphere.

The accepted history goes something like this: While traditional media companies stumbled through a technological shift, a bunch of freethinking, self-published writers used platforms like Blogspot, WordPress, and AdultFriendFinder to democratize journalism. Voices outside the political and media establishment entered the fray and disrupted the discourse. They forged direct relationships with their audience, crowdsourced information, and hosted dialogues and debates with their readers. They weren't media professionals, either—these "citizen journalists" were salt-of-the-earth constitutional lawyers, doctoral candidates, financial analysts, and unemployable loners like Will Menaker. They did *not* play by the rules.

In fact, they were portrayed as the Young Turks of the Old Media Empire—rebels overturning a stuffy and moribund status quo. The analogy holds up well enough, given that the insurgents who created modern Turkey went on to ally with the Central Powers in World War I and carry out the Armenian Genocide.* We shall find our blogging heroes also had a penchant for shitty politics and mass slaughter in the Middle East.

For it was indeed around this time that the media led the country into war with Iraq, again on false pretenses, through breathless and selective reporting about Saddam's possession of WMD, a total fabrication that was used to justify invading Iraq for a second time, building a new American empire, and creating ISIS.

The Forerunners

Ben Smith, editor in chief of *BuzzFeed*, celebrated this "golden era of political blogs" in a 2013 postmortem:

> I was a local politics reporter in New York, and I'd spent the 2004 campaign obsessed with its central, vital new media

---

* Allegedly.

> outlets—Josh [Marshall]'s liberal *Talking Points Memo*; Andrew Sullivan's pro-Bush *Daily Dish*; *Little Green Footballs* and the other conservative sites that punctured Dan Rather's killer story on Bush's National Guard service. Matt Drudge was already the grandfather of that ecosystem; Sullivan had, legendarily, gone down to Miami to seek his advice before launching his blog in 2000.*

Once Drudge lent Sullivan his lucky pair of calipers on this fateful occasion, the new age was under way.

Matt Drudge—credit where it's due—was indeed a key founder of the blogosphere and therefore a transformational figure in the history of American journalism. He is also an inveterate racist, paranoiac, and creep who wears a dumb little hat all the time, and is therefore a continuation of the Old Media style. Embracing the tabloid principle of "I'll take credit if it's true and claim free speech if it's not," Drudge struck gold in the late 1990s. He skimmed enough e-mails from demented Republican readers to finally stumble onto a genuine scoop: the Monica Lewinsky affair. (*Newsweek* had the story, too, but decided not to run it.) Twenty years after Watergate, the political scandal of the year was published by a man who looked like a real-life Max Headroom. Out of nowhere, the *Drudge Report* had beaten the mainstream press to a story that struck at the heart of the president's dignity, stature, and ability to effectively prey upon interns. Just as the mentally ill Chicago hospital custodian

---

* Ben Smith, "My Life in the Blogosphere," *BuzzFeed*, January 28, 2015, https://www.buzzfeed.com/bensmith/this-is-my-blog?utm_term=.ufPmlmOWb#.ghlvQv9mY.

Henry Darger did with art, Drudge inaugurated a new form of outsider journalism.

But for every new gumshoe reporter who took up this new style of "blogging," the Internet generated a hundred more citizen-pundits gushing unearned confidence and horrid opinions. The story arc that unified all the bloggers was 9/11, the reign of George W. Bush, and the Iraq War, which virtually all of them supported—from conservative techno-glibertarian ghouls like *Instapundit* to "liberals" like Democratic consultant John Aravosis. And so the political blogosphere emerged first and foremost as an interminable, half-decade-long symposium made up of insecure, overeducated armchair generals, dipshit philosophers, and racist crackpots, each one playing a pint-sized Thucydides, possessing none of the wisdom and all the side effects of venereal disease.

One such crackpot was the next guy on Smith's list, *Little Green Footballs,* otherwise known as Charles Johnson (not to be confused with redheaded goon Chuck C. Johnson, a different piece of shit who showed up later on). Johnson's blog was a great example of the baby-boomer-warmonger type: a ponytailed website developer and accomplished jazz guitarist, Johnson was one of the most vicious and repulsive "critics" of Islam occupying the early Internet, spewing every anti-Muslim trope in circulation and tirelessly advocating that America treat the Islamic cancer with good old-fashioned radiation.

In a twist that makes him an even better model-blogger specimen, Johnson got woke around 2009, became a staunch opponent of conservative "wingnuts," and meticulously deleted and even *altered* many of his old posts that clashed with his new liberal brand. Like George Lucas re-editing *Star Wars* every five years, Charlie was simply retouching his work to reflect what the posts *should* have said.* This included scrubbing the scores of times he or any of his devoted readers ranted about "Islamofascism," seethed over the Ground Zero Mosque, or referred to American pro-Palestine activist Rachel Corrie—killed by an Israeli bulldozer in 2003—as "St. Pancake."† Good guy.

Anyway, Little Green Charlie is a perfect manifestation of the self-promotional and protean qualities of the blogosphere. He illustrates how someone whose "work" was once approvingly cited in the manifesto of white supremacist mass murderer Anders Behring Breivik can successfully pivot to being *against* genocide.

Another one of Smith's blogging titans was Andrew Sullivan, once upon a time the biggest pro-war pundit in the game. He was an exception to the blogger-as-outsider origin story: Sullivan rose to prominence as the boy-wonder editor who ran the *New Republic* during the height of its "welfare-queens-are-selling-your-children-crack" years. (But he also advocated for gay marriage, so, who's intolerant now, bitch?) It was Sullivan who published the infamous excerpts of race scientist Charles Murray's *The Bell Curve,* which blamed America's racial inequality on black people's IQ levels. To this day, Sullivan still insists Murray's theory is onto something and urges his fellow intellectuals to teach the controversy.

---

* Jonathan Dee, "Right-Wing Flame War!" *New York Times Magazine*, January 21, 2010.

† "Fact Check: Johnson's 'Saint Pancake' Comment Stood for Years," *Diary of Daedalus* (blog), December 7, 2011, https://thediaryofdaedalus.com/2011/12/07/fact-check-johnsons-saint-pancake-comment-stood-for-years/.

His blog began as yet another cranky right-wing LiveJournal until 9/11 and the buildup to Iraq, which catapulted so many of these humps into the ranks of the War Bloggers. The war liberated him, and so many others, from any remaining threads of sanity, and it earned Sullivan a loyal audience of equally pretentious psychos. A sample frothing, written a few days after 9/11:

> The middle part of the country—the great red zone that voted for Bush—is clearly ready for war. The decadent left in its enclaves on the coasts is not dead—and may well mount a fifth column.*

Another:

> When you look at the delighted faces of Palestinians cheering in the streets, we have to realize that there are cultures on this planet of such depravity that understanding them is never fully possible. And empathy for them at such a moment is obscene. But we can observe and remember. There is always a tension between civilization and barbarism, and the barbarians are now here.†

Sullivan's prose was always tidier than that of his American comrades, but the unhinged paranoia in that first quote and the bloodthirsty jingoism in the second are prime examples of what was teeming in the minds of all these oafs: History, capital *H*, had

---

* Andrew Sullivan, "ABC News' John Miller Likens Bin Laden to Teddy Roosevelt," *Daily Dish*, September 19, 2001 (1:59 a.m.).

† Andrew Sullivan, "Today," *Daily Dish*, September. 11, 2001 (9:46 p.m.).

arrived, and these dorks were eager and willing to chronicle it, maybe even shape it, and deluded enough to think that their razor-sharp polemics would help guide Bush's wrecking ball across the Middle East.

But just like Little Green Johnson, Sully did an about-face in 2006, around the time America's campaign of death and misery in Iraq was getting a little too sloppy, and Pvt. Charles Graner & Co. were discovered reenacting their favorite scenes from *Salò* at Abu Ghraib prison. Always one with a wet, sticky finger to the air, Sullivan's ideological weathervane proved slightly more attuned than those of the native Yanks. As such, he distinguished himself by turning against the Iraq War a full two weeks before everyone else did. Over the next several years, he moved from panic to doubt to full-on antiwar ideology, just in time to embrace the shimmering, redemptive light of Barack Obama's candidacy in 2008. (Full disclosure: a young Brendan interned at the *Dish* in 2013, after this woke transformation took place.)

Though Sullivan still clung to dumb, Third Way, Simpson-Bowles–style domestic politics, he'd become a vocal opponent of everything from the drug war to interventions in Libya and Syria to support for Israel. He never did kick that race science, though, even as Obama's #1 fan. And sure enough, recent years have once again soured Sullivan's brand as he dispenses five-thousand-word essays about how Plato would likely blame Donald Trump's election on college kids who want to assign pronouns to your yogurt.

As you can probably tell, the blog era was a shot in the arm for the conservative commentariat. But there were still some lefties and liberals in the mix—least of all the progressive hub *Daily Kos,* founded by a young clone of Gilbert Gottfried named Markos

Moulitsas. *Kos* was, for its time, a firebrand site that raged not only against the nightmarish Bush machine but also the weak Democrats who enabled barbarism at home and carnage abroad. The bottom-up "Netroots Nation" was hailed as the liberal answer to the resurgent right-wing media embodied by Fox News and their newly recruited army of bloggers like *RedState*'s Erick Erickson, *Town Hall*'s vaudeville dummy Ben Shapiro, and the *Gateway Pundit*, aka the *Dying Pundit*, a racist invalid who refused to let his myriad terminal illnesses affect his output of xenophobic tirades. *Daily Kos* fought fire with fire and spoke not for the liberal party elites but for the ponytailed, guitar-owning grassroots.

But once Obama took office, *Kos* went soft. By the 2016 primary, the site had been completely assimilated by the Borg of the Democratic Party, launching illiterate polemics against anyone who dared to endorse or support the tepid New Deal Democrat Bernie Sanders over the bloodless, focus-grouped, corporate-approved campaign of Hillary Clinton. His brain broken by the 2016 primary, Moulitsas himself now spends his days screaming in the street about "the alt-left" and writing screeds *against* the distinctly progressive goal of universal health care so as to more effectively exterminate the lumpenproles who voted for Trump: "Be happy for coal miners losing their health insurance. They're getting exactly what they voted for," he wrote in December 2016.*

---

* Markos Moulitsas, "Be Happy for Coal Miners Losing Their Health Insurance. They're Getting Exactly What They Voted For," *Daily Kos*, December 12, 2016.

The Young Turds

Once the template had been erected by pioneers like Drudge, Sullivan, and Moulitsas, the gate swung open and the children of Yog-Sothoth were now able to pass through into our realm. Thus a fresh generation of unnameable, social-climbing heels were free to parlay their vile ambition and Internet savvy into full-blown careers promoting war and the interests of the unspeakable Elder Gods that spawned them. The New Blogs had arrived.

Perhaps the most successful of these has been the dynamic duo of Matt Yglesias and Ezra Klein, who have gone on to found one of the most influential and infuriating new media properties, an entity you know as Vox.com. Ezra and Matt were liberal wunderkinds who used the nascent medium of blogging to talk about serious issues in "a post-9/11 world" in a hip, cool way, while still getting a pat on the head from teacher. For instance, Ezra would always make sure to lard his blog with *Manchurian Candidate*–style recitals of how "kind," "talented," "smart," and "reasonable" people like David Brooks were. And why wouldn't these mooks look up to someone like Brooks? Ezra once described his fellow wizard wonks as "free-traders, interventionists, fiscally conservative, market-friendly peeps." How do you do, fellow kids?

Still, united by their mutant neoliberal politics, he and Matty had different styles: where Ezra was always a soft touch, Yglesias started his blogging career as a liberal hawk, trying to get the coveted *Instapundit* link, which meant shitting on weenie human rights types, fantasizing about a war between Islam and the West, and daydreaming of Gitmo prisoners being shot while trying to escape.

(Wink, wink.) But for both Ezra and Matt, supporting the Iraq War was never a moral failing on their part but an analytical one. For them, the main question was not "Should the United States invade a country that poses no threat to us and had nothing to do with 9/11?" but was "If we oppose a war every reasonable person supports, how could we possibly look 'Serious'?" In a 2004 blog post, Ezra explained his support for the war like this:

> As Matt and I have both noted in the past, part of what sent us towards the hawk camp was that, without much historical context for what war means, we simply evaluated the arguments (and sadly, that means the spokespeople) for the two sides. In that calculus, becoming a hawk seemed not just warranted, but unavoidable. That's not fair to the doves and not fair to the Democratic party, and while we (hopefully) won't make the same mistakes again, it's really incumbent that the anti-war wing funds a media savvy opposition (instead of protests organized by subsidiaries of Maoist groups [read: ANSWER]) so future generations aren't turned off by the absurdity of their spokespeople.*

In their own words, they really had no choice. Camp Hawk was where all the "serious" jobs were! You see, if the antiwar side had developed a "savvier" media shop in 2002—instead of simply turning out millions of ordinary people into the streets, all over the world—there's a good chance they could have given Matt and Ezra

---

* This post is now offline, but Will has a screenshot.

the "historical context" that war involves mostly senseless cruelty and slaughter. People like M&E generally regard everything to be a matter of "optics," and at the time, being against the War on Terrorism would look very, very bad! To their finely calibrated moral and aesthetic compass, the hippies and dopey Marxists shouting in the street looked absurd and clueless, whereas Donald Rumsfeld, Fred Barnes, Bill Kristol, and Paul Wolfowitz looked dignified, smart, and fuckin' hot to boot.

His credentials as a smooth-brained cretin established, Ezra went on to write for legacy progressive publications like the *American Prospect* (where he wrote in favor of single-payer health care),* became *WaPo*'s resident "wonk," and finally founded Vox.com (where he wrote *against* single-payer health care).† Matty, meanwhile, managed to con editor after editor into allowing him to write books about things he knew less than nothing about. Reinventing himself as a business expert, a foreign policy expert, a Bangladeshi factory expert,‡ and a housing policy expert, he eventually joined Ezra to found a website whose purpose is to "explain the news."

Of course, along the way, they both wrote lukewarm mea culpas for their Iraq days. Ezra came up with this rather novel excuse: "Rather than looking at the war that was actually being sold, I'd invented my own Iraq war to support—an Iraq war with different

---

* Ezra Klein, "The Health of Nations," *American Prospect*, April 22, 2007.

† Ezra Klein, "Bernie Sanders's Single-Payer Plan Isn't a Plan at All," *Vox*, January 17, 2016.

‡ Matthew Yglesias, "Different Places Have Different Safety Rules and That's OK," *Slate*, April 24, 2014.

aims, promoted by different people, conceptualized in a different way and bearing little resemblance to the project proposed by the Bush administration. In particular, I supported Kenneth Pollack's Iraq war."* In other words, Ezra was like the autistic boy in the finale of *St. Elsewhere,* the war he supported existing only inside his little snow globe. Meanwhile, Yglesias also blamed Kenneth Pollack's 2002 book *The Threatening Storm*—the *Turner Diaries* for the liberal-hawk set—as just being too damn convincing! In 2017, Yggy smugly announced that he is now "against all war," having had this elementary moral breakthrough at thirty-six years old.

It can't be stressed enough that Matty and Ezra's subsequent media careers were direct rewards for their shallow, dim-witted support of the biggest foreign policy disaster of our lifetimes (so far). To join the op-ed industry, like *La Cosa Nostra,* you become part of an elite brotherhood of murderous sociopaths who dress like shit and eat too much. You have to "get made," and in This Blog of Ours, you pledge your support to a disastrous and completely unnecessary war the same way mafia thugs burn the likeness of a saint, except instead of a card it's a city full of people.

But enough about the wonder twins: their friend on the right, Megan McArdle, provides an even more nauseating portrait of the upward trajectory of those who fail in all the right ways. McMegan began her blogging career writing under the pseudonym "Jane Galt," named after one of the characters in Ayn Rand's dystopian classic *Atlas Farmed: 1984.* As a recent college graduate in 2001,

---

* Ezra Klein, "Mistakes, Excuses and Painful Lessons From the Iraq War," *Bloomberg View,* March 19, 2013.

Megan—like most of us—figured out if you couldn't get the job you wanted on Wall Street or in "management consulting," you could at least spend your hours at the shitty job you *do* have posting on the Internet.

However, unlike normal people stealing time for wholesome things like playing fantasy football, downloading music on LimeWire, or watching pornography, Megan spent her time as "Jane Galt" on her even more insufferably named blog, *Asymmetrical Information*, where she was free to share thoughts such as why she had no opinion on gay marriage, even though it's still bad:

> This should not be taken as an endorsement of the idea that gay marriage will weaken the current institution. I can tell a plausible story where it does; I can tell a plausible story where it doesn't. I have no idea which one is true. That is why I have no opinion on gay marriage, and am not planning to develop one. Marriage is a big institution; too big for me to feel I have a successful handle on it. . . . Is this post going to convince anyone? I doubt it; everyone but me seems to already know all the answers, so why listen to such a hedging, doubting bore? I myself am trying to draw a very fine line between being humble about making big changes to big social institutions, and telling people (which I am not trying to do) that they can't make those changes because other people have been wrong in the past.*

---

* Jane Galt, aka Megan McArdle, "A Really, Really, Really Long Post about Gay Marriage That Does Not, in the End, Support One Side or the Other," *Asymmetrical Information*, April 2, 2005, http://archive.today/DL3ja.

And why the Iraq War will absolutely *not* cost "trillions of dollars":

> Anyone who's sat through a budget meeting knows that almost everyone overestimates their successes, underestimates their costs; it's easier to go back for money later, when you can wave a nice hunk of sunk costs around, than say up front that you think whatever it is you're proposing will be expensive as hell. But trillions? US GDP is roughly $10 trillion. [Eric Alterman] is saying that over the long run, this war is going to cost us at least 20 percent of GDP. That's nuts, and it's not the first time I've seen those sorts of numbers around. Reality check: the entire US military budget is in the range of $350b.*

In the same post, Megan estimated the death toll to be in the "hundreds" and also blamed critics like James Galbraith for not taking into account the "positive effects" of a war such as increased consumer confidence. As J. Galt, Megan cultivated a unique blogging style that perfectly matched being stupid with thinking your readers are stupid. She would loudly announce her disinterest and lack of expertise in a given subject, and then opine on it at length. Her specialty was laundering hard right-wing free-market ideology behind bullshit "on the one hand, on the other hand" hedging in an unbearably twee writing style.

None of this would be particularly noteworthy amid the sea of

---

* Jane Galt, aka Megan McArdle, "How Much Is the War Going to Cost?" *Asymmetrical Information*, March 23, 2003, https://archive.is/GSvUm.

mediocrity that was the early blogosphere. However, Megan truly distinguished herself when she called for Iraq War protesters to be literally beaten in the streets:

> I'm too busy laughing. And I think some in New York are going to laugh even harder when they try to unleash some civil disobedience, Lenin style, and some New Yorker who understands the horrors of war all too well picks up a two-by-four and teaches them how very effective violence can be when it's applied in a firm, pre-emptive manner.*

Damn, that is some asymmetrical information! When she was eventually called out for these ghoulish sentiments, Megan claimed she was only talking about *violent* protesters and then brought up the volunteer work she did at Ground Zero and her high school boyfriend who was killed on 9/11 by Saddam Hussein.

After a few years of arguing that poverty is caused by inner-city types not getting married and skewering all forms of social welfare, government regulation, consumer protection, child labor laws, and anyone who opposed the Iraq War with her snark-tastic wit, McMegan got the call: she was leaving the minors to join the *Economist* as a professional blogger. Like Yglesias, she would then go on to blog at the *Atlantic,* covering "business and economics" amid personable, relatable digressions about the dangers of using a Kindle in the bathtub, the problems caused by being tall, having a cold,

---

* Jane Galt, aka Megan McArdle, "Bring It On," *Asymmetrical Information,* February 13, 2003, https://archive.is/Yitep.

and waiting on line for Apple products. As in her Iraq War days, she used her Criswell-like powers to advise readers "not to panic" about the sudden contraction in the financial markets in 2007. When the entire market collapsed a year later, she dutifully churned out post after post absolving bankers of any criminal or moral wrongdoing and blaming the crisis on government regulation and the individual avarice of greedy homeowners and borrowers.

Following her stint at the *Atlantic*, Megan fused with the Kuato-like mutant that was the *Daily Beast/Newsweek*, where her biggest hit was a four-thousand-word meditation post–Sandy Hook on why we should condition children to do human wave attacks on mass shooters:

> I'd also like us to encourage people to gang rush shooters, rather than following their instincts to hide; if we drilled it into young people that the correct thing to do is for everyone to instantly run at the guy with the gun, these sorts of mass shootings would be less deadly, because even a guy with a very powerful weapon can be brought down by 8–12 unarmed bodies piling on him at once.*

Her writing was so smart and good that she got a massive salary boost at *Bloomberg View*.† There, she now shares Patrick Bateman–style reviews of kitchen appliances in between columns about how

---

* Megan McArdle, "There's Little We Can Do to Prevent Another Massacre," *Daily Beast*, December 17, 2012.

† As of publication, McMegan has failed upward again, this time at the *Washington Post*.

hundreds burning to death in an inadequately regulated firetrap isn't really anyone's fault because they could have eventually died some other way.

McMegan is truly the perfect model for new media #successwin: she shows that demonstrating an adequate level of contempt for your readers, the universe, and the human race will get you noticed and hired by people even more evil than you, i.e., the demons who own and run media companies. After all, Matty and Ezra now run their own company at *Vox*, and why shouldn't they? They're smart, serious, know more than you do—and, what's more, they hold the keys to your new career as an opinion explainer.

The Blogger's Code

We've been tough on the grand tradition of American media, but honestly, almost any part of its history was probably light-years better than the garbage that emerged in the mid-2000s. A couple good eggs pushed through: *Gawker* was a genuine example of an independent media company that skewered basically all the right assholes sucking off the political and media establishment. Sprinkled elsewhere were plenty of fresh non-bougie bloggers, many of whom managed to leverage careers out of their writing, and good on them.

But for the most part, the blogosphere was a league of pathetic, repulsive morons who mastered a technology every child knows how to use and used it to become the new generation of talking heads thanks to credulous media executives at CNN and the

Washington Post. Don't take it from us—take it from human toothbrush Ezra himself, reminiscing on his early blog, *Tapped*: "Without *Tapped,* there would certainly be no *Vox.*" As Ben Smith pointed out, besides the radical Left, virtually all factions' boats were lifted by a tide of shit: led by right-wing blobs like Erick Erickson, smug careerists like Yglesias, and just plain dumbasses like Chris Cillizza, the blog boys piloted journalism into a newer, even more idiotic frontier of toxic hackery.

The fresh, sleek presentation of new media—held together with fictitious venture capital and sponsored content like "Why It Takes a Pregnant STEM Graduate to Build the Perfect Missile" or "What My Poly Triad Breakup in Big Sur Taught Me about the Smooth, Low-Key Independence of the Ford Focus"—is a departure from journalism's humble past, but no one can deny that it retains the goofiness of its origin. The future may hold horrors for the blogmasters, whether it's everyone finally figuring out that no one buys stuff from online ads, young people seeking op-eds further left than Steny Hoyer, or a disastrous accidental reply-all e-mail wherein every single editor accidentally sends *hentai* to senior White House sources. Indeed, the night is dark and full of blog fails, and these thought leaders are waddling into an uncertain world that may spell the end of their line. But as it is written in *The Blogger's Code* (2004):

> *Let ye wander into lands unknown*
> *Let commenter and blogger moan*
> *Post in light, post in dark*
> *From Ebaum's World*

All th'way to Fark
We know not what the road betrays
But only in our blogging ways
Let ye screen illuminate the path
Before ye wife unleashes wrath

Blog forever, and in honor

CHAPTER FIVE

CULTURE

We can forgive a man for making a useful thing as long as he does not admire it. The only excuse for making a useless thing is that one admires it intensely. All art is quite useless.

—OSCAR WILDE, *THE PICTURE OF DORIAN GRAY*

Why Donald Trump and Jeb Bush Should See Hamilton

—REBECCA MEAD, *THE NEW YORKER*

For a long time people had a crude but basically correct understanding of culture's relationship to politics: Marx's idea that the "superstructure" of society—law, morality, and culture—arises out of the economic meat grinder hidden underneath, the "base." This rough version of the theory gets criticized as simplistic, and to be fair, it is: there are all kinds of inputs and outputs that determine culture, and there's plenty of good criticism of this bastardized version of Marx. Still, as far as we're concerned, it's always better to err on the side of *this* crude theory than to go in the opposite direction, the For Dummies version of Antonio Gramsci: the idea that a nation's culture is self-reinforcing and affects all other walks of life, so if you change the culture, you can change the political reality. To quote the Italian Communist himself, "Ingredienti migliori, cultura migliore, Papa John's."

The taste of Gramsci-lite won a lot of people over during last the few decades, trading away material and economic analyses for an overwhelming focus on culture. But this approach comes from the generally bad side of 1960s radicalism (incidentally, the only part that survived). It was embraced by middle-class hippies whose demands were not material and collective but aesthetic and individualist—which, once you smooth off the edges, is just libertarianism. We know this because almost all those baby boomers grew up to become square, greedy marketing consultants for UBS who also happen to smoke weed while they binge-watch *Westworld*.

That's because capital has no problem assimilating pop-cultural rebellion and antiauthoritarian imagery. In fact, that stuff creates all kinds of new markets, new consumers, new suckers. All the cultural modes of resistance slowly turned into marketing categories, and the brave hippie dipshits of the sixties left us with an even more powerful money machine, totally compatible with social liberalism and openly unafraid of the militant but always shrinking left-wing movement. In the absence of real political power, liberals and lefties stumbled into a pathology where we only hold power over—and wage struggles for—the realm of fantasy.

That would be bad enough, but ever since The Incident in 2016, some of us have tumbled through the looking-glass. People have fallen victim to the same forces that so addled James Woods's character in Cronenberg's *Videodrome*: having become obsessed with the hypnotic imagery inside the TV, they began to hallucinate in their waking hours, confusing fiction for reality and vice versa. They went beyond fighting over TV and film and fantasized that they were, in some form, fighting *inside* the world created by TV and film.

Hillary became Khaleesi. Trump became Voldemort. And as the *Videodrome* synthesizers hummed along, some dark conspirators took a giant videotape and shoved it into Lawrence O'Donnell's pulsating chest and said, "death to Trump, long live the new flesh." Along with him, wide swaths of the liberal and left spectrum have become the video word made flesh, the evil wavelengths of the TV eating away at their brains until they believe not only that culture is the way to achieve social justice but that *Game of Thrones* or Harry Potter itself *is* social justice.

This is not to say people shouldn't seek comfort in art, in TV, in movies. It's the only way to not go mad! But, in our view, do it *knowing* what you're doing is fun and aesthetic, not militant and subversive—it's never going to substitute for real political action. It may make you feel better to watch a show that's calling out Trump, or oppression, or our podcast—but if you stop there, you're demobilized as a political actor. Again, between half-assed Marx and half-assed Gramsci, it's better to go with the former: of course being in control of what is "cool" in our culture is a kind of power, but it's one that liberals increasingly rely on in lieu of actual politics, to the detriment of politics—and culture, and cool people.

On the other side, for the culture warriors of the Right, a death grip on power maintained through gerrymandering, voter suppression, etc., will never be enough to give them what they truly crave: popularity, celebrity, and the admiration of the same cultural elite they despise. Despite witnessing a rich pedigree of reactionary artists in the early twentieth century (Céline, Ezra Pound, Leni Riefenstahl, Hanna-Barbera), the contemporary American right-winger is congenitally incapable of being funny, entertaining, or interesting in any of the ways art demands, relying instead on ham-fisted sentimentality and self-abasing ressentiment. The paradox is that the further their liberal enemies get from holding real power—the more they rely on the symbolic and pop-cultural—the *worse* they get at the very things that built liberal cultural hegemony in the first place. Libs find themselves aping the shittiest habits of their right-wing culture-war opponents. As this war on culture progresses, both the general public and cultural elites ask less of art and reduce their interests to a checklist of "good points" or "progressive portrayals" while ignoring anything that doesn't superficially conform to the immediate political conversations of the day.

Don't get us wrong—we're not *against* state censorship, as long as we're in charge of it. After Chapo Year Zero, we'd probably leave most film, literature, music, and television alone and focus instead on censoring things that are truly evil, like TED Talks; Malcolm Gladwell books; the study of economics, philosophy, and journalism; and the just plain boring things like poetry, dancing, and plays. After all, Soviet Russia and Communist China kept a close watch on artists, while our own CIA funded plenty of literary magazines and writers' workshops to nudge the culture in the right direction—so if you can't beat 'em, join 'em.

It's time that we turned the tables on the ruling class and prescribed our own correct Chapo cultural revolution. Hopefully you, too, can become a Chapo-certified Free Thinker™ or at least understand the references that form the broad outlines of our cryptic inside jokes and long-winded "ironic" remarks that allow us to get away with making so many Polack jokes.

Film Products

The legendary Soviet film director and theorist Sergei Eisenstein once said that "American capitalism finds its sharpest and most expressive reflection in the American cinema." This remains as true today as when Sergei made his classic film about the most powerful and biggest battleship ever. Film remains a potent vehicle for ideology. However, if film can be harnessed to transmit capitalist ideology, then it stands to reason that it can also be used to send more subversive messages. Indeed, the revolutionary potential for film is limitless, and movies have played an integral role in firing our imaginations and forming our worldview. Here are a few of the most important.

The Matrix

All we can say is, "Wow!" 1999's *The Matrix* is probably the most important movie ever made. Even if it was just the film's badass gun murders and high-flying kung fu, it would have its place in the Western canon. But at its heart is a moral more valuable than possibly any work of art ever: that being on the computer is cool, sexy, and important. Instead of reverting to the trope of computer users as sedentary slobs who avoid the real world, the Wachowskis showed us that the only way to see the truth is to be so online that you could die from it. Simply put, take the red pill and get back on the keyboard and mouse!

The Matrix Reloaded

They say you have only one chance to make a first impression. Well, that may be true, but you also have two chances to make a second impression, and it's twice as important, because it's like a first impression times two. That's doubly true for *The Matrix Reloaded*. The sequel may actually be *more* important, as we're introduced to three major characters who show us the sexy dark side of the computer. First is the Merovingian, a French pervert who represents all French people who are online. He makes some sort of chocolate cake that makes a woman nut, which is a metaphor for mutual masturbation on Skype. The next two, of course, are the Twins. Let's put it this way: You've seen albinos. You've seen white guys with dreadlocks. You've seen identical twins. You've even seen white three-piece suits. But have you seen them all together? The Twins shifted the realm of what was possible in the minds of viewers. It's no mistake that only six years after *Reloaded* and the Twins, George W. Bush stepped down as president of the United States. Good art makes you think. Great art makes you act. Enough said.

The Matrix Revolutions

All good things come to an end. But they live in our minds forever. Coming out the same year as *Reloaded*, the third installment completed this biblical fable. Honestly, we don't remember this one too well. There were some new robots. The Merovingian is there, but doesn't cause any nutting. The important thing is that Neo dies doing computer stuff, becoming a hero forever. This is a metaphor for doing a dangerous stunt on a livestream that kills you.

The Animatrix

If The Matrix series constitutes one whole Koran, *The Animatrix* is the definitive *hadith*. While the films focus on knocking viewers' socks off with sick action set pieces that act as amuse-bouches for the main course of philosophy and even cooler action scenes, *The Animatrix* does not ease the viewer in, for this simple reason: for all the Matrix series's revolutionary ideas and concepts, it was still trapped within the confines of Hollywood films, which are produced by degenerates and idiots who think filmgoers are as stupid as they are. Series-defining features like the Twins and the Colonel Sanders guy were put off till much later, as the repulsive freaks who constitute Tinseltown's leadership could barely handle them.

Their powerful ignorance, however, did not extend to the art of anime. Producers like Joel Silver found the medium too complex and powerful to dig their hideous claws into, allowing *The Animatrix* to flourish. In *The Animatrix*, viewers are treated like adults and shown vignettes about a guy who runs really fast, a robot who's a slave, and other ideas that would simply be too much for Hollywood to allow in a conventional film. If you think you can handle it, dive in, and *Dōitashimashite* (Japanese for "you're welcome").

Television Products

We all love our stories. They give us something to look forward to at the end of the day and something to talk about with family, friends, and coworkers. Television is the younger cousin of film, but one that has perhaps even greater power to shape minds, as we invite it into our very homes. Long gone are the days when an entire family had to gather 'round the tube to watch *Amos 'n' Andy* or the Kennedy assassination. Now there are so many channels, so many content providers, and so many damned good programs that it's hard to know where to start. Since we like to think of America as one big family, and the TV as the thing that unites us all, here are stories about a couple of criminal families that represent America while remaining fiercely united.

The Sopranos

To truly understand America in the twenty-first century, one must imbibe the entire run of *The Sopranos* as it was originally intended to be seen: in one seventy-hour sitting. In *The Sopranos,* creator David Chase gave us a host of characters who represent the grand archetypes of our culture and where it was headed at the dawn of this new millennium. In patriarch Tony, we have the cheap and nasty criminal sociopaths who would inherit the world, namely Trump and those who voted for him. If you want a vision of the future, just imagine America wearing a soiled bathrobe, sullenly staring at a bowl of Honeycomb cereal in a gaudy exurban McMansion. As a counterpart to Tony's criminal depressive, we have wife and mother Carmela, who represents the complicit suburban petit bourgeois, happy to live a life of comfort funded by blood money in between charity bake sales held to assuage the phantom pangs of a nonexistent conscience.

Hovering above everything like a black, odious cloud of shit is the sour and berating matriarch Livia, who represents the crushing weight of olds on the American psyche, sapping us of joy, independence, and any chance to escape our history. As a corollary to all our collective efforts to overcome the psychological damage done to us by Livia (i.e., all previous generations), there is Dr. Melfi, Tony's therapist, who represents the ultimate and final failure of educated, cosmopolitan liberals to meaningfully confront—let alone reform—evil. Throughout the run of the series, Melfi's attempts to treat Tony serve only to help him manage his criminal empire more efficiently, making her at best an enabler and at worst an accomplice.

Finally, in the Soprano children, we see the two paths laid out for the millennial generation. In Meadow we have the "success daughter," a high-functioning and ambitious striver with a superficial interest in social justice who is well adapted to the world of neoliberal hegemony. In AJ, we have the great American failson, a figure uniquely ill suited to the times. AJ is lazy, petulant, insouciant, and one Howard Zinn book away from realizing how fucked-up shit really is. He is the ur-figure for what would eventually become the podcast listener and host.

Sons of Anarchy

Some hour-long dramas follow great men who walk the line between good and evil, while others show people who are forced to commit immoral acts due to brutalizing circumstances. But only one show is about a hugely stupid man whose good acts always result in evil because the soft spot on his skull never hardened. That show is *Sons of Anarchy*, and that towheaded imbecile hero is Jax Teller.

The heir to a family of motorcycle dunces, Jax leads a gang of sex perverts, delinquent dads, and murderers known as SAMCRO (Sons of Anarchy Motorcycle Club Redwood Original). His late father, John, bequeathed him a semi-flattened carton of Kool XLs, a twin bed, and a series of journals that turn out to be unreadable libertarian drivel about how he tried and failed to make a vroom-vroom club for grown men but his vision was ruined.

While this may seem like utter nonsense, it actually has deep cultural meaning: after 9/11, the small and silver screens were dominated by tales of good and evil like *The Lord of the Rings*, *Spider-Man*, and *24*. We clutched these simple narratives about highly competent protagonists who exhibited extraordinary abilities, selflessness, and flawless moral compasses like security blankets while being fed easily digestible footage of air strikes and easy military victories. Their stories buttressed our self-narrative as a benevolent empire giving back what we'd gotten from rank evildoers. However, as the Iraq and Afghanistan Wars grinded into bloody, unwinnable occupations, the economy sputtered, and everything turned out to be much more complicated than we wanted to believe in our deepest moments of agony. Simple hero's journeys would no longer do.

We needed a new type of good guy, one who fucked up so badly that everyone around him died, who fought hard despite not knowing what he was even fighting for. Someone who talked the talk and walked the walk, right into a field of rakes. That man was Jax Teller, a stand-in for both our then president, with his own father issues, and ourselves. SAMCRO's dusty Northern California hamlet was a microcosm for the world at large, with the good townspeople and the snarling black and brown gangs who sought to upset the Sons' murder-based economy. American exceptionalism became the bike buffoons' indecipherable moral code.

You cannot understand America without understanding *Sons of Anarchy*, and you can't understand *Sons of Anarchy* without understanding America.

Literary Products

Literature—it's our name for books that are full of emotion and make-believe as opposed to facts and reason. Inexplicably, these works filled with lies, nonsense, incorrect political ideology, and not a single graph or chart are still venerated as vital parts of our culture. Once a book is deemed important by the literary elite, it enters what's known as "the canon." You're probably familiar with the *Simpsons* parody versions. In many cases, elevator schematics hold up better than these "classics,"* but if you learn the plots of a few of them, you can likely hold your own at Chapo speed dating sessions.

Moby-Dick by Herman Melville

Roundly regarded as the single greatest American novel ever written—if not the best of any nation's output—*Moby-Dick* is about a young man who decides to go whaling for a few years because he's depressed, and going to sea is an act of self-care. He travels from New York to New Bedford and meets a guy named Queequeg from the South Pacific Islands who practices cannibalism and is really

* See page 220 (where the Elevator Products section begins).

good at harpooning whales. They spend a night together in a hotel room, fall in love, and join up with a ship called the *Pequod*, which is captained by a madman named Ahab who is hell-bent on pursuing his vendetta against a legendary white whale who bit his leg off.

With a winning plot, featuring a battle between an unstoppable monster and the lunatic who wants it dead, you'd think the book would be a page-turner. But after setting up the central conceit, it goes on for about four hundred pages describing the different kinds of knots and ropes that are used on a whaling vessel. It's pretty boring, but if you want to sound smart, you can bring up the fact that it's chock-full of homosexual themes. For instance, the narrator begins the novel by stating that he "set out to sail a little," which was a nineteenth-century euphemism for cruising. Pretty much the entire thing is just metaphors for being gay. Back then you had to be on a boat to have sex with a man, so that's the subtext for the whole book, which is summed up in its deceptively simple opening line: "Call me gay."

Middlemarch by George Eliot

Set in the fictional English Midlands town of Middlemarch, this book is a sprawling and epic portrait of provincial life and social change in nineteenth-century Britain. Though written in the Victorian era, it has many of the hallmarks of modern novels, such as its refusal to conform to a given style, dense literary and even scientific digressions, and multiple and diverging points of view. So, yeah, our main takeaway is that George Eliot was a really great writer and probably didn't get the recognition he deserved while he was alive.

The Adventures of Huckleberry Finn by Mark Twain

Race relations in the nineteenth century were strained, to say the least—that is, until great strides were made in the field of white guys ironically using the n-word. In his classic satire of life on the mighty Mississip, Samuel Clemens—who posted under the screen name "Mark Twain"—created a comic masterpiece: a tale of a rapscallion named Huck and his friend who will be referred to in these pages as "Jim" and certainly nothing else. By realizing that a white author could get away with using racial slurs provided he didn't use his real name and used the slurs only to point out that racism is bad, Twain created a distinctly American art form that endures to this day.

The Great American Novel by F. Scott Fitzgerald

In his book *The Great American Novel,* F. Scott Fitzgerald set out to write something that would be taught in American high school English classes forever, and in so doing created an indelible portrait of life during the "Roaring Twenties." The book is about a reclusive millionaire bootlegger named Gatsby, who, despite his money, spends most of his time as beta orbiter to a woman named Daisy whom he met in Army training.

Gatsby spends his money on lavish parties he doesn't attend at a house he bought across from Daisy's so he could impress her, specifically in a way that didn't involve making eye contact or conversation. Fitzgerald's book is about the dark side of the American dream, suggesting that we can all be alpha players if we use advanced PUA tactics. But in reality, only a few of us are going to be born "great" enough to consistently score with straight-up tens. The rest of us are left to beat off, ropes against the current, jacking off ceaselessly into the past.

Anything by William Faulkner

It doesn't matter which one you read, because they all take place in a terrible part of Mississippi where every once-proud family is riven with secrets about incest, interracial children, grotesques, suicide, financial ruin, abortion, or some combination of all of the above. Faulkner's books often feature "stream-of-consciousness" and "nonlinear" narration, which are the techniques serious authors use when they're trying to make fun of the mentally handicapped.

To Kill a Mockingbird by Harper Lee

Much like the work of Faulkner, *To Kill a Mockingbird* is another great book about how the Depression-era American South was a rich, magical place full of colorful characters. With Maycomb, Harper Lee created an unforgettable portrait of a "tired old town" in an America gone by. Maycomb is the kind of place where you wish you could have spent the halcyon days of childhood summers with Jem and Scout, whiling away the days indulging in high jinks down by the ol' fishing hole with loveable town drunk Bob Ewell, playing pranks on Tom Robinson or rounds of mini golf with man-child shut-in Boo Radley. *To Kill a Mockingbird* isn't just a book for kids, though—it also has lots of lawyer jokes that adults can enjoy, too.

Naked Lunch by William S. Burroughs

"Agents of unconsecrated insect semen corporations repent! The control you seek is in your own prolapsed asshole!" Who can forget the first time they read those immortal lines in William S. Burroughs's classic book about shooting heroin into your dick? *Naked Lunch* was the first American novel to not be a novel or "readable" in the traditional sense. Extremely controversial upon its initial publication, it faced a long battle against censorship for violating nearly every social convention of the day in its depiction of drug addiction, homosexuality, and *actually, for-real* killing your wife. *Naked Lunch* follows William Lee, the literary alter ego of Burroughs, through a series of loosely connected vignettes or "routines" as he travels to the fictional country of "Interzone," a place where it's okay to have sex with teenage boys. In addition to expanding the American literary consciousness around issues of drug use, murder, and ephebophilia, it also has a long and rich legacy of inspiring people to start rock bands and do heroin.

Dune by Frank Herbert

Probably the most important book ever written outside of the Holy Koran, Frank Herbert's *Dune* is a sprawling sci-fi epic about a war between two powerful galactic dynasties who battle for control of a planet that's too spicy. The planet in question, Arrakis, is a giant political allegory that contains the universe's most precious resource—except instead of oil, it's the cum of giant space worms. The worm-cum is called "spice," and it's both an energy source that bends space and an *extreeeemely* dope fucking hallucinogen. *Dune* created a huge universe with dozens of characters and long story arcs carried out over a whole series of books and helped inspire the sci-fi/fantasy megafranchises of today, like Harry Potter, Star Wars, and *Game of Thrones,* which all borrowed heavily from *Dune* in that they're also thinly veiled calls for their young readers to martyr themselves in a holy jihad against a corrupt and decadent American empire.

Blood Meridian by Cormac McCarthy

See the book—It is thick—Sentences short—Landscapes bleak—Glanton gang—Doing genocides to Indians—War is good—Yonder bald man is large—Universe is indifferent eternal violence—It is also good—The men tell the women to read the book—Sometimes they don't—Then men cry

White Noise by Don DeLillo

This book is good to know about because it's a satire of academia, and if you want to pursue a postgraduate degree, it's important to keep this one in your back pocket so you can impress your peers by being "in" on the joke about how they're full of shit and their career choice is pointless. The book follows professor Jack Gladney and his family in the small midwestern college town where they live. Gladney is a professor of "Hitler Studies," and though the book was written in the 1980s, DeLillo had an uncannily prescient vision of the "irony occupations" that would become prevalent in the twenty-first century. The book channels a lot of the broadly felt anxieties surrounding consumerism, mass media, divorce, and train derailments that cause huge leaks of airborne chemicals that undergird so much of modern American life.

Garfield: His 9 Lives by Jim Davis

There are many classic *Garfield* collections that belong in the American canon, such as *Garfield: Bigger Than Life*, *Garfield: The Big Cheese*, and *Garfield: Origins*, but *Garfield: His 9 Lives* warrants special consideration for the astonishing and groundbreaking questions it poses about the very nature of literature and authorial intent. Organized into ten short stories, each differing wildly in content, style, setting, and tone, the book completely recontextualizes the Garfield character and, by extension, the reader's shared experience of Garfield the Cat. *His 9 Lives* contains meditations on the creation of cats and the role of large, surly cats throughout history, as well as stylistic digressions into detective fiction, slapstick, and William S. Burroughs–style cut-up experimentation. The effect can be jarring, and indeed, *His 9 Lives* was savaged by critics upon its first release, but with time it has come to be recognized for the work of genius it truly is.

Painting Products

Paintings get a bad rap for being boring, but it is nevertheless important for you, the callow and stupid reader, to embrace the visual arts, as communion with paintings opens you up to unique experiences and sensations. It also trains the mind to notice small details and contemplate what lies beyond the surface.

Bal du moulin de la Galette (Pierre-Auguste Renoir, 1876, oil on canvas, Musée d'Orsay)

Impressionists sought to capture moments in time through swift brushstrokes, wet-on-wet intermingling of colors, and careful attention to natural light. Renoir's masterpiece depicts a moment in the Montmartre, a district where working-class Parisians would dress up, drink, and dance. The patrons are dappled with blotches of light shining through the canopy, imparting a vivid sensation of motion to the tableau as the eye imagines trees swaying over the dancing couples in the middle distance and the young raconteurs in the foreground.

Like all impressionist artworks, *Bal du moulin de la Galette* invites the viewer to imagine these patrons naked if he or she gets bored. The figures depicted all appear fairly attractive—the fluid brushstrokes obscure any imperfections, much like an Instagram filter—and it is not beyond the bounds of belief to think they could all strip off and have an impromptu orgy, considering the sexual mores of urban Paris at the time. Careful observers will note that Renoir inserted fellow painters Pierre Franc-Lamy and Norbert Goeneutte in the lower right as voyeurs nursing glasses of grenadine, dreamy expressions on their faces, almost certainly picturing Monet being beaten with a riding crop.

Guernica (Pablo Picasso, 1937, oil on canvas, Museo Nacional Centro de Arte Reina Sofía)

The destruction of the small village of Guernica during the Spanish Civil War heralded a modern horror that the entire continent of Europe would soon be acquainted with: terror bombing. Pilots sent by Nazi Germany and Fascist Italy to aid Franco's Nationalists reduced the town to rubble, killing hundreds of civilians and paving the way for ground forces to march in amid the chaos. Having received a commission from the Republican government to create a work of art for the Spanish display at the World's Fair in Paris, Picasso responded to this atrocity with a twenty-five-foot mural in the cubist style depicting the experience on the ground during the raid. Employing simple lines and a black-and-white palette, *Guernica* is a raw depiction of humans and animals panicking, suffering, suffocating, and dying through the horrors of war. The skewed perspective—a hallmark of cubism that seems in this case to perhaps dehumanize the figures, or to emphasize their captivity—and the incorporation of newspaper print indicted contemporary viewers for being passive observers to human suffering, an early critique of the mass media that remains strikingly relevant in the digital era.

Guernica has resonated through the ages as the most profound visual encapsulation of man's inhumanity to man in the era of mass communication and mechanized warfare. It has also resonated as a hugely erotic work of art. The emphasized hands and feet on the wailing human figures are an obvious nod to fetishists, but what makes Picasso's masterpiece truly revolutionary is his incorporation of highly sexualized cartoon animals whose bodies intersect with other figures. Modern-day vore, furry, and even hentai subcultures can all trace their lineage back to *Guernica*, which, along with Betty Boop, *Li'l Abner*, and George Orwell's *Animal Farm*, was for millions of people the World War II–era precursor to DeviantArt.

Four Darks in Red (Mark Rothko, 1958, oil on canvas, Whitney Museum of American Art)

Rothko's later work consisted of abstract "multiforms," canvases featuring little more than overlapping layers of color. He once said of his paintings, "I'm interested only in expressing basic human emotions—tragedy, ecstasy, doom, and so on—and the fact that lots of people break down and cry when confronted with my pictures shows that I *communicate* those basic human emotions."

Four Darks in Red, with its horizontal swaths of black and red hues, presents no conventional narrative to interpret but instead exists as a form in and of itself, containing its own meaning through imparting an experience to the observer. The central, primal emotion aroused by this experience is horniness, as the observer cannot help but be sexually excited by the bold colors arranged in rectangular shapes whose juicy borders and low-key thiccness call to mind throbbing red cocks and big-ass pussies. The real subversion of *Four Darks in Red* is that, despite its lack of recognizable human figures, no one can observe this composition without getting so profoundly horned-up that they lose their job.

Grey Lines with Black, Blue, and Yellow (Georgia O'Keeffe, 1923, oil on canvas, Museum of Fine Arts, Houston)

These are some pretty flowers. The colors are interesting and nice. Not much else to say about them.

Elevator Products

We've discussed film, television, literature, and painting, but are you ready to get higher than you've ever been before—and then seamlessly and safely travel right back down again? Then prepare yourself to appreciate an often overlooked form of human creative achievement: elevators.

Thyssenkrupp

You're on the fifty-third floor of a skyscraper overlooking downtown Raleigh, North Carolina. Your partner and infant twins (one girl, one boy) are on the forty-seventh floor. You hear a loud bang. The building shudders. Ceiling tiles fall. Smoke fills the room. Sirens wail. You come to on the floor and realize that another 9/11 has happened. How do you get to the ground floor safely and efficiently? You could take the stairs, but that's a lot of stairs. That's when you remember that this is a Thyssenkrupp building. You pick yourself up and march to the elevator bank and hit the down button, secure in the knowledge that a century of German engineering has ensured that even in the event of catastrophic architectural failure, goddamn it, these elevators will make it to their destination.

The doors open. The building lurches and groans as you step

into the car. The doors shut so quickly that you wonder whether you've died and entered a conveyance to hell, because surely only the devil himself would be capable of achieving such a short door-closing time.

People in the car are crying, diarrheaing themselves, that sort of thing. But your eyes are glued to the state-of-the-art LED display showing each floor you pass by, an amenity you've come to expect from a modern elevator. The only thing more shocking than the accuracy of the digital indicator is the celerity with which this car is approaching the ground floor.

You exit the car into the lobby and run outside the building. Your partner and kids are there. They also took a Thyssenkrupp-manufactured elevator to escape. You embrace them. You look up and discover that the building isn't actually collapsing. It was all a false alarm, a fake 9/11 meant to test the integrity of the building's elevators in the event of a national emergency. The Thyssenkrupps passed with flying colors. You and your partner look deep into each other's eyes. No words are needed. Your look says it all: "I will always love you. Thyssenkrupp, whose elevators are unsurpassed in terms of efficiency and reliability, will keep us together, no matter what."

Otis

The year is 2152 AD. The world's resources have been nearly exhausted. A corrupt ruling class maintains control over the last scraps of the earth's bounty through elaborate systems of violent repression. Your "name," were such a thing conceivable to you, is Quantum-291. You have no parents, no heritage that you know of. You have not been permitted to have a personality. You have known no life but servitude to the Directorate as a menial laborer in the cobalt mines. There is very little cobalt left in this vein. Each week you and your dozen fellow laborers must show quota. The one who mines the least is sent to University. No one has ever returned from University.

Last week Quantum-285 was sent to University. You knew him for nearly two cycles. He was the closest thing you ever had to a "friend." He once risked his life by sharing his 500 milliliters of soy slurry with you when you were being punished with starvation for glancing at the Overseer's console.

You were bred to know nothing, but now you have learned something. Now you have a rudimentary understanding of kindness, which has led you to conclude that something like "justice" exists. Using subtle gestures and miners' argot, you are able to communicate this concept to your fellow Quantums.

At the appointed time, you collectively turn your laseraxes and cyberdrills on the Overseer. The man you once watched personally zap a miner to death for singing off-key at grueltime now begs for his life. It brings you nothing but pleasure to watch his life force be torn into tiny shreds of flesh.

Klaxons blare. Reinforcements are coming. The only hope for you and your nascent freedom force is to exit the mine as fast as possible. The odds may be long, but if you can get aboveground in time, you and your comrades have a chance to scatter across the surface and spread your revolution to drone warrens throughout the Cryptosphere.

You and your fellow rebels make a break for the mine elevator. You press the button. You wait. You hear the elevator creak and groan as it descends toward your floor. The Klaxons grow louder. Overseers from surrounding tunnels are closing in on you. You press the button again and again and again. Your comrades start to panic. What's taking so long?

Psychoblaster shots fizz around the corner. The elevator finally settles on your floor. The doors slowly open. You shove your way in and slam the S button. The elevator shakes. Panicking, you hit the button over and over again. The doors start to close but stop a quarter of the way. Beyond the elevator doors, a team of black-suited Troublers has appeared, their psychoblasters aimed squarely at you. You wave good-bye to them, expecting the doors to close at that second, saving your life and the lives of your friends.

The doors don't close. You are blasted into darkness. When you awake, you and all your colleagues will be sentenced to 1,500,000 millennia of mentotorture for your little insurrection, an unspeakably excruciating penalty that will last one hour in real time and can—and will—be renewed at the whim of the magistrate who sentences you.

In the last moments before you succumb to the blaster's effects, you yell, "I am not a Quantum! I am a Tesla Model 663, and I am *alive*!" Then you fall to the floor, your circuitry shorted. The last thing you see before losing consciousness is the infernal word etched at the bottom of the elevator shaft: OTIS.

Schindler

This is an okay elevator. Not great, but not bad, either.

So ends the brief survey of what you will be allowed to read, watch, and ride after the coming revolution.

But every manifesto must contain both a positive platform and a negative critique, and it's to the latter we now turn. Though we pride ourselves on our general tolerance of deviant, revisionist, and counterrevolutionary cultural output, there are certain kinds of decadent formalism that can and will be eradicated from the landscape when Chapo commissars take their stations in government. Atop the pile is one figure in particular, a renegade hyena who preaches a disgusting creed of logic, braininess, and love for truth.

The Sorkin Mindset

Liberals, having sold out decades ago and laid the welcome mat for a new era of right-wing domination, have long retreated into realms of fantasy. In the aftermath of the 2016 elections, they've disappeared into cultural cosplay more than ever before—and no one has done more to sculpt their virtual reality than the master of the monologue, the king of quips, the ayatollah of argument: Aaron Sorkin.

Everything shitty about libs, from their smugness to their worship of decorum to their embarrassing rhetoric of "resistance," is arguably Sorkin's fault. From humble beginnings as a cheesy but not terrible playwright, Sorkin has come to dominate the popular imagination, and has done more to poison American political culture than anyone since D. W. Griffith. Sorkin's preeminence in the world of political drama testifies to the destitution of American culture. Let's survey the damage.

To Sorkheads, of course, his dialogue is electric, his characters are memorable, and his narrative voice is bold and unmistakable. Another Hollywood weirdo with far more talent, Quentin Tarantino, once gave this stunning quote to *New York* magazine:

> Now, the HBO show I loved was Aaron Sorkin's *The Newsroom*. That was the only show that I literally watched three times. I would watch it at seven o'clock on Sunday, when the new one would come on. Then, after it was over, I'd watch it all over again. Then I would usually end up watching it once during the week, just so I could listen to the dialogue one more time.

The fact that Tarantino—a man heralded, rightly or wrongly, for his command of snappy banter—felt comfortable praising Sorkin's dog-shit show for the same strengths shows how far America has strayed from the light. Through some alien brain virus, people have learned to regard Sorkin's Adderall-fueled schlock as the gold standard.

In fact, *The West Wing* is the Rosetta Stone of every stupid thing that contemporary liberals have come to believe. Many of us in Chapo were impressionable kids when *West Wing* first came on, and as we grew older and slightly less stupid we went through the natural progression of disgust with this show: first, we realized that the way things worked on *The West Wing* wasn't the way they worked in the real world; then we realized things had *never* worked that way; then finally we realized things *should not* work that way. That would be horrible. It would be a gaudy, unending pageant, full of self-obsessed blowhards saving the day not through radical change or real moral courage but with shitty zingers and face-to-face bloviation.

The show was, however, an instant hit among those enjoying the twilight of the Clinton years, when it first lit up the screens of content, sated middle-class families who felt that basically all the problems had been solved. Once George W. Bush slithered into office in 2000, the show took on a new purpose as a liberal fantasia, presenting an alternate universe where everything was fine and the Yosemite Sam Republicans were put in their place with catty banter and speechifying. But then, after eight years of evil with the Bush administration, the Sorkinites got their wish with Obama, a real-life Jed Bartlet: a Nobel Prize–winning commander in chief who was eloquent, academic, and presidential, and who ate dog.

And sure enough, the show telegraphed every single failure, error, and misapplication of power in the Obama years. Why? Because the people in charge finally got their chance to play out their fantasies of being characters on *The West Wing*! In so doing, they ran straight into the maw of real politics, power, and ideology. Anyone who may once have believed in the Sorkinverse discovered, if they were paying attention, that the person who had the most data at their fingertips and owned the other person in the debate did not automatically win.

To give an example of the show's diseased politics: In season five, episode twelve, Toby Ziegler voices the dreamy prose of Sorkin's pen to make a bold, brave, and moral case to cut Social Security. The whole episode chronicles his effort to form a commission that will reduce benefits and save the program from an (invented) financial doomsday. And were it not for the CHUDs of the Freedom Caucus who spoiled it for John Boehner in 2011, President Jed Obama would've gotten his Grand Bargain, which had been designed to obliterate the American welfare state to appease the honorable Republicans on the other side of the aisle.

And that, in closing, is the scariest thing. This shit went from pages on a cokehead's laptop to a network TV show straight to the Obama administration: Obungler came onto the scene in 2004 with his Sorkinesque DNC speech about how there's no "red or blue America," then campaigned on "bipartisan," nonideological solutions to the unambiguously partisan and ideological onslaught of right-wing America. And we don't even need to go into all the ways the administration pursued the stupid neoliberal fantasia that *West Wing* characters such as Toby preached, like getting everyone from both sides into the same room to hash out the most reasonable solution to a divisive problem. Hell, there's even an episode in which Josh Lyman has a beer summit, à la Henry Louis Gates Jr., at the White House with a Republican with whom he trades facts and bromides about gay marriage.

This reality-bending curse latched on to Obama's would-be successor in 2016 when Hillary Clinton's rolling calamity of a campaign took every page from the Bartlet manifesto. Take note: In season three, episode fourteen, as Bartlet runs for reelection, Toby Ziegler counsels the president before a crucial televised debate: "Make this election about smart and not; make it about engaged and not; qualified and not. Make it about a heavyweight—you're a heavyweight, and you've been holding me up for too many rounds." Bartlet goes on to own the shit out of the folksy, dumbass, Jeb Bush–style yokel, and the president is reelected in a landslide. Why? Because he was smarter than the other guy in the debate.

You could see how ill-equipped to operate in the real world this liberal adulation of the office of the president was once the long reign of Democrats in the twentieth century came to an end. As soon as they slipped out of power, their ideology—their mythology, really—left nothing in the toolbox that would get them back in. They were equipped only to keep *inheriting* power; as soon as

NEWS SHOW
ARF CHOMP ARF GULP MUNCH
GULP ARF CHOMP SMACK
MR. NEWSROOM!
PLEASE CEASE YOUR EATING ACTIVITY AND MAKE YOUR ATTENTION KNOWN TO YOUR NEW ASSISTANT
WILL THEY BE ASSISTING ME BY PROVIDING THE DUMPLINGS I ORDERED AN HOUR AGO?
IF YOU DON'T BEHAVE YOU'LL BE "ASSISTING" YOURSELF AT HOME WITH YOUR HAND FOR A MONTH
MURROW GOT DUMPLINGS WHENEVER HE WANTED
IF YOU DON'T HAVE DUMPLINGS WHAT DO YOU DO?
IF IT PLEASES THE NEWS MAN, I HAVE A DEGREE IN SOCIAL MEDIA SNAP CHAT FROM AN IVY LEAGUE...
IGNORANT SWINE!
YOU DISHONOR THE NEWS WITH YOUR FRIVOLOUS FEMALE PURSUITS!
I COVERED THE GULF WAR AND THE CLARENCE THOMAS HEARINGS!
I ASK FOR DUMPLINGS AND YOU BRING ME THIS DUMPY AIRHEAD WITH NO UNDERSTANDING OF THE GREAT NEWS OF THE WORLD!
MEMO TO MURROW: TODAY'S GREAT NEWS IS HAPPENING ON 4 CHAN AND /POL
4 MAN? SLASH POL?!? SLASH MY THROAT WITH SHARP WINDS OF THE WEST!
ASSISTANT WOMAN, TEACH THIS OLD AND POWERFUL PUNK SOMETHING...
THE PRESIDENT HAS JUST TWEETED THAT YOU ARE A "VERY DISHONORABLE OLD FOOL"...
...WHO DOES "COUNTERFEIT HEADLINES" ABOUT HIS INVOLVEMENT...
GIVE ME MY NEWS DESK
I AM GODDAMN NEWSMAN!!!!

Excerpts from the never-before-seen manga written by Aaron Sorkin, ジャーナリズムのヒーロー：エラーの悪魔への攻撃 (*News Hero: Attack on Demons of Error.*)

they lost it, they had no tools or vision for getting it back. Watching *The West Wing* twenty years on, you realize that as the Democrats lost each and every municipal, state, and now national office, their self-perception as heroic Jed Bartlets and C. J. Creggs and Josh Lymans only grew deeper and more convinced. The further liberals got from power, the further they delved into fantasy and the more they appropriated Sorkin's pithy banter, letting events pass by, letting history shove their heads down the toilet for a swirly scored by the tinkling notes of Thomas Newman.

It is decreed by the Chapo Central Committee that, seeing as Sorkin's ethos completely and utterly missed the mark and led to a bunch of greasy, half-literate tristate area slobs occupying the decorated halls of the White House, Sorkin should be legally mandated to remake his entire series—same dialogue, same camerawork, same music—but swap out the liberal philosopher kings for people like Donald Trump, Michael Flynn, Stephen Miller, and the Hamburglar.

VIP TV

Sorkin, too, however, is a symptom of a bigger problem.

At the turn of the twentieth century, America had a problem: polio, sure, but, even worse, the lack of opportunities to laugh at the high jinks of a fat guy and his hot wife. Yes, there was vaudeville, but the scarcity of theaters where you could spend an evening chuckling at a portly gentleman and his incongruously attractive spouse as they threatened each other with violence left millions of rural Americans out of the fun. There had to be a better way.

Thanks to the spirit of American ingenuity that never allows a need to go unanswered for too long, that better way was unveiled in 1928 when inventor Philo Farnsworth debuted his all-electric televisual network. "With this miraculous device," Farnsworth said, "Americans from coast to coast will be able to observe the merry antics of a rotund workman and his comely helpmate from the comfort of their own homes!"

The device caught on among a public hungry for scenes of domestic gaiety between comically mismatched romantic partners, and by the 1950s, the television set was a staple appliance in the American home. Each night, families would settle in and enjoy wholesome programs like *The Honeymooners, Texaco Presents: The Oaf and the Dish,* and *The General Electric Obesity Hour*. While situation-based comedies such as these remain a mainstay of television, over time, increasingly sophisticated audiences began to demand a greater variety of programming, such as rigged game shows, blackface shenanigans, and the adventures of horny doctors, horny lawyers, and horny cowboys. None of it was *good,* mind you, but it wasn't supposed to be. Real, challenging art was to be found in books and at the theater (the latter is still boring, though). TV was for shutting off your brain and basking in a sea of banal amusement after a hard day's work. This upset highbrow nerds like FCC chairman Newton Minow, who famously called television a "vast wasteland" in 1961, but most Americans were happy to reply, "Shut up, bitch, *Car 54, Where Are You?* is on."

And so, network television existed for decades in a state of tranquil stasis: sitcoms, soap operas, lawyer shows, doctor shows, cowboy shows. The only major changes were that the cowboys eventually turned into cops and networks began to allow actual minorities to appear on-screen. Suddenly, in the 1990s, there was a burst of innovation. Chief among the new types of programs was the "reality show," which, by the turn of the century, was threatening to consume civilization with increasingly dystopian offerings. The low overhead and huge viewership of lurid, vérité programs like *Billionaire Bride Auction* and *Celebrity Ape Hunt* ate into the market share of scripted programming. For a moment, it seemed the networks had found a solution to the rising competition from cable. They seized upon this silver bullet, and it looked as though soon the only things on prime-time TV would be public executions and Regis Philbin. But then *The Sopranos* happened.

David Chase's show, broadcast on the pay-cable channel HBO and thus freed from the content and commercial restrictions of the broadcast networks, combined the thematic and character complexities of literature with the mature, stylized visual content of film on the small screen. Narratives stretched across seasons, not just episodes. Clear-cut resolutions were replaced by lingering ambiguities. Characters underwent the sort of personality transformations that would have alienated previous generations of TV audiences, who cherished the soothing familiarity of archetypes. It turned out that television wasn't just a place to zone out and chuckle at cloddish husbands; it could produce art just as challenging and thought-provoking as any other medium.

Inspired by Chase's accomplishment, a whole generation of creative heavyweights set to the task of putting their own mark on the tube. The next two Davids, Milch and Simon, empowered by an HBO hungry to replicate the overnight phenomenon that was *The Sopranos*, created a pair of shows, *Deadwood* and *The Wire*, respectively, that failed to match *The Sopranos* in viewership but achieved posthumous critical canonization. It was AMC, a network that had previously specialized in showing old Hollywood movies to a small audience of nostalgic geriatrics, that really managed to copy the *Sopranos* formula with Matthew Weiner's *Mad Men* and Vince Gilligan's *Breaking Bad*. These shows achieved levels of popularity and critical acclaim that had never been seen before, and certainly not on basic cable. Television got so good, in fact, that it wasn't long before the dominant opinion among cultural tastemakers was that TV had surpassed film as the most vital popular narrative art form.

With books deemed a dying medium and cinema dominated by superhero pablum, it wasn't unreasonable to seek intellectual and creative stimulation elsewhere—and with TV outlets and streaming services multiplying like toadstools after a rainstorm, the sheer volume of serialized storytelling meant you don't have to leave your couch to find it.

This line of thought soon calcified into its own orthodoxy, with its own shibboleths: we're living in the "Golden Age of Television," don't you know, and the shows we watch aren't just shows, they're Prestige programming. The premise of this cant was to assure people that they didn't have to bother with challenging literature or indie cinema; television could provide all their cultural vitamins and minerals without their having to strain their eyes or leave their houses.

This Golden Age of Television heuristic was created and enforced by a new class of television critics who got their start in digital media outlets that, not coincidentally, sprang into being just as TV shows started getting "good." The explosion of Web traffic in the early 2000s led to a huge demand for content, and media reviews were the cheapest, easiest content to crank out. This created a recap economy, in which poorly paid content creators put out instant reviews of television shows hours after they aired, and gave the people who'd just watched those shows space in the comments section to have the conversations about those shows they weren't having with their nonexistent real-life friends. It was a faulty critical model (books aren't reviewed by the chapter, films aren't reviewed by the act), but it was perfect for the audiences of those websites: bored cubicle workers with Internet connections at their desks and no energy to do anything after work but sit down and watch television. Everyone involved in this cycle, from the website owners to the writers to the eager comment-section dwellers, had a vested interest in framing TV as the most important, most thoughtful, most artistically satisfying medium.

It wasn't long after *Prestige TV* became a buzzword that the term began to be defined less as embodying any particular standard of "quality" (which, after all, is a mostly subjective concept) and more as a collection of surface-level signifiers. These proved much easier for networks and producers to replicate than the lightning in a bottle that was *The Sopranos*—so that first generation of prestigious television gave way to a second wave that mimicked the content, style, and mood of its forebear without the point of view or craftsmanship. Shows like *House of Cards* and *Westworld* sport the high production values and cinematic atmosphere that signify Prestige but the characters, dialogue, plots, and themes of a tryhard freshman fiction workshop. Even higher-quality shows like *Fargo* strain so hard to be legible to reviewers by underlining each episode's themes so that they can be pointed out in recaps that feel contrived and flat. Even the best of them tend to recycle tortured male antihero tropes and rely on genre conventions because audiences love a guy with a gun.

And more enervating than the cynicism and relentless sameness of Prestige TV is the way the concept serves as a brainlessly proud monument to techno-capitalist exhaustion. Viewers, worn down by draining and unfulfilling work lives, socially and emotionally isolated, priced out of expensive movie theaters, attention spans and reading ability obliterated by the informational overload of the Internet, reach for any available confirmation that zoning out on the couch counts as cultural enrichment. Poorly paid content-mill providers are charged with providing that confirmation, treating every new show with decent production values and an angsty protagonist as an Important Commentary on Our Times.

This is ice cream for dinner. Television is an inherently middlebrow medium, and dressing up shows with blockbuster production values and Big Social Themes won't change that. Aside from surreal ten-minute comedies shown at 4:00 a.m. on *Adult Swim* and stuff by brand-name weirdos like David Lynch who made their reputations in film, there's no real TV avant-garde. Movies and books, as one-off, take-it-or-leave-it pieces of art, can challenge and provoke in ways that TV shows, always angling for viewers to tune in to the next episode so they get renewed, simply can't.

The idea that a thing like Prestige Television exists spreads the poisonous notion that these shows, which at this point are blurry copies of the original article, are sufficient cultural nourishment. We need better than that if we're going to learn how to live in the burning circus tent we call twenty-first-century America. Instead of taking what's offered to a demoralized, dispirited population by people whose precarious livelihoods require us to keep watching and sounding off in the comments and calling it "good enough," we need to demand to live in a world where the burdens and alienations of modern life are lightened, allowing us to watch movies in the morning, read books in the afternoon, and critique TV after supper.

Gaming

Prestige TV may seem benign, but if we don't resist its siren song, the grim end result will be something far worse. We speak, of course, of gaming, a growing strain of entertainment that jettisons all pretensions to artistry, theme, or even craft in fav~~or of catering to the basest instincts of an increasingly slothful and sadistic citizenry, a citizenry every day rendered more vile, more hateful, more incapable of basic social function by the mindless b~~

This is Virgil Texas (Gamertag: Obamacare) speaking. I've hacked into the printing press to delete this shameful anti-Gamer tirade written by my revisionist colleagues. In its place is a brief manifesto about the purest, most revolutionary form of art, courtesy of me and Felix (Gamertag: Professor_Headshot).

~~GREETZ~~

Congratulations, you've "scored." You've "pounded beers" and "had sex" after "winning state." Your life has peaked after batting the game-winning slam dunk and fingering the tight end of the opposing sportsball squadron. As you deplete your brain cells and bodily fluids for a few moments of base skin pleasure, engaging in a series of high-five-style hand slaps whilst listening to brain-dead hip-hop about being a "player," your imagination grows too feeble to anticipate the years beyond your wasted youth when you will slip into an inexorable mental decline from years of brutal blood-sport and testosterone supplement abuse and your nasty children will quibble over who gets your vintage Toyota Matrix. When you reach the end of your finite supply of orgasms, having long since become immobile due to the idiot's brew, perhaps you might realize in your last few flashes of lucidity that you could have been a different type of person had you spent your peak years in discipline, self-denial, and constant practice. Perhaps you could have been an artist, a nomad, a connoisseur, a genius, a freedom fighter, a warrior. Perhaps you could have taken a name that struck fear into the hearts of strangers in every realm you wandered. Perhaps instead of some mewling crotch spawn left to defile your legacy, your progeny could have been an avatar that would have granted you immortality in the Cloud.

Perhaps you could have been a Gamer.

Being a Gamer first and foremost means being a well-rounded intellectual. A Gamer embodies the classical Greek ideal of a human being: an athlete, an aesthete, a philosopher. Like Jean des Esseintes, the Gamer spurns vulgar bourgeois society to devote their life to total immersion in high culture. From their aerie, the

Gamer consumes art that speaks to all of the human condition. The Gamer explores notions of identity and genetics in *Metal Gear Solid*, destiny and duty in *Halo*, and speed and sexuality in *Sonic the Hedgehog*. The Gamer uses controllers and keyboards as keys to the universe, achieving a level of interaction with essential texts that book readers could only ever dream of.

The Gamer does not eschew nongaming social interaction. When not challenging one another in teamchat, Gamers take to the agora of the message board, from which the highest intellectual activity of the past three decades has emerged. They usually debate games as art, sport, and life on the boards, but their wisdom is also seen in famed Off-Topic threads such as "Asshole Parents Won't Accept Rent in Bitcoins," "Who Invented Blow Jobs?," and "Short Men Shouldn't Have to Pay Taxes."

The rest of the world anguishes over menial tasks like office small talk and family get-togethers so much that there's an entire genre of writing dedicated to how they should confront their mean uncle or not humiliate themselves at the watercooler. They mope about fuckbois on Tinder, asexual representation in *Riverdale*, and whether they should tip their therapist. They've created a world of supposed creature comforts that they're too self-conscious and neurotic to even enjoy, their fleeting moments of leisure alternating between self-flagellation and self-importance.

In comparison, the Gamer exists in his own space, separate from the dirty terrestrial confines his siblings, cousins, and classmates imprison themselves in. One doesn't need a guide to arguing politics on Thanksgiving if one just shuffles out of one's room, loads up a plate, and hurries back to *Orc Theme Park Tycoon* without once making eye contact. Why make an existential crisis out of dating app travails when one could just forgo all romantic ambitions? Why twist oneself in knots over how one comes off to a coworker if one can just avoid a job altogether? While normies toil in the brutal purgatory they've created for themselves, the Gamer moves freely between virtual nations, unharmed by a doomed society's jagged edges.

A Brief History of Challenging Everything

The first computer game was coded by Ada Lovelace, history's first programmer, for Charles Babbage's Difference Engine. *Cholera Quest* was a modest success in Victorian London and sparked a debate over whether women should be allowed to be computer programmers, a controversy that rages to this day.

Graphical games emerged during the Cold War, when technicians poached from the ruins of the Nazi war machine by the RAND Corporation designed such rudimentary games as *Tennis for Two, Tic-Tac-Toe,* and *Missile Command.* The latter was famously enjoyed by John F. Kennedy, arguably our first Gamer president, who used lessons gleaned from *Missile Command* to defuse the Cuban Missile Crisis, telling Soviet premier Nikita Khrushchev, "The only winning move is not to play." This, of course, was a lie, as the real moral of the game was to spawn nukes to build up an overwhelming first-strike capacity and take out your opponent's missile installations before he has a chance to retaliate, a lesson quickly internalized by a young Pong aficionado Gamer named Henry Kissinger.

The video-game gap between the US and the USSR widened in the 1970s and early '80s, when consumer capitalism produced the Atari 2600 and *Pac-Man,* a game that simulated rapacious gluttony, while state Communism produced the Autotraktor Konsole and *Tetris,* a game that simulated the repetitive and futile drudgery of manual labor.

In consumerist societies, pricey home-gaming systems proliferated until the mid-1980s, when overspeculation on health-drop derivatives caused the infamous video-game crash of 1983. Out of the ashes emerged the Japanese, who established the modern video-game console model with the Nintendo Entertainment System. From then on, Gamers were treated to an unbroken string of leading-edge consoles, each more eye-poppingly advanced than the last: SNES, Sega Genesis, N64, Xbox, the fucking Sega Saturn that you got for Christmas when you *said* you wanted a PlayStation. For an industry driven by the recommendations of the man at the video-game store who said you would want this, gaming has experienced a nearly unparalleled rate of innovation, bested only, perhaps, by gun manufacturing and pornography.

Yet for every two steps forward, gaming has taken a step back. Modern gaming is more immersive, more profound, and more challenging to the Gamer's intelligence and reflexes than it has ever been. But the industry is blighted by unfair pay-to-win models; loot-box scams; invasive DRM schemes; preorder rip-offs; DLCs substituting for core content; abusive labor practices toward developers, testers, artists, and voice actors; and players getting banned from Xbox Live for total bullshit reasons. Misogyny and racism run rampant in the darker corners of the gaming world. Your opponents are winning because of lag. Scott won't let me play, even though it's a two-player game. How should the moral Gamer act when faced with such endemic malignance? How shall we purge these noxious elements so that we as Gamers may finally reach Outer Heaven?

Ready Player Fun

The Gamer acts, first and foremost, by gaming. For all its longevity and cultural impact, gaming as an art form is arguably still in its infancy. As with any virgin mass-media culture, the contours of its evolution will be dictated by a mixture of capital and the expectations of its audience. As a digital medium with many forms and genres—mobile gaming, browser gaming, eSports, big-budget titles, indie games, RPGs, simulations, etc.—gaming is evolving rapidly in several different directions, and the proliferation of developer tools and a relatively low barrier of entry for game creators means new ideas, mechanics, and experiences can be introduced by nearly anyone with a computer and free time. And if the blogosphere, social media, and self-publishing have taught us anything, it's that most of this new "outsider" content is sure to be spiritually and intellectually uplifting.

Looking forward, virtual reality is the next logical development in human culture. Much like the way you can't pay your phone bill without going online anymore, one day you'll handle all your transactions by putting on a VR outfit, walking to a virtual bank, and interacting with a nine-foot-tall Spyro the Dragon as a woman with big breasts. Virtual reality will consume all other art forms. Instead of reading a physical novel or e-book in the meatspace, we'll suit up and open a virtual tome. Once we've fully shed the fetters of our corporeal bodies, we'll finally be able to attend digital concerts, meet up at digital bars, and make digital love with one another, all on VR servers like *xXx_DarthBudBundy_xXx's Room* [*FULL Married with Children RP ONLY*].

Will this brave new world be any better than our current one? For the answer to that question, you'll have to buy the second edition of this book. Until then, we at Chapo Virtual House say, "Long live the New Flesh, same as the Old Flesh!"

CHAPTER SIX

WORK

In capitalist society, work is the cause of all intellectual degeneracy, of all organic deformity.
—Paul Lafargue

Work sucks, I know.
—Blink-182

ost Americans despise their jobs, yet suffer from a species of brain worm that makes them believe work is inherently virtuous. America thinks of itself as a come-to-play-every-day, lunch-pail kind of nation, possessing intangible strengths like "coachability," "instinct," and "a century or so of a free labor supply" that have made us rich, powerful, and the envy of the world. The American Work Ethic sets us apart from flashy, hip-hop-style, vacation-taking European countries and other players with raw, natural ability, like China. We keep our heads down, never complain, and grind every day. That's how global economic champions are made.

And, for some reason, we take for granted that for the majority of the precious handful of decades we're alive, we'll be making money for someone else, doing something we'd rather not do. Not only do we resign ourselves to this fate, we want nothing more than to make sure everyone else is roped into the assembly line as well. At the bottom of our stomachs we hate our bosses, but we dream of someday becoming them. Political theorists call this "fake consciousness," and there is no faker friend than your boss, no faker crew than your workplace.

So why do we put up with it? The answer lies in a shared set of national beliefs about work and how it sets us free. The first key myth in this psychology is a timeless classic you'll hear from warehouse managers, boomer dads, and Joe Biden: "Work builds character." Here's the latter at the 2012 Democratic National Convention, quoting his own dad:

> Dad never failed to remind us that a job is about a lot more than a paycheck. It's about—[applause]—it's about your dignity. [Cheers, applause.] It's about respect. It's about your place in the community. It's about being able to look your child in the eye and say, Honey, it's going to be okay, and mean it, and know it's true. [Cheers, applause.]

Usually when people invoke "character," it means some combination of grit, patience, determination, ingenuity, focus, self-discipline, and empathy. And sure, these are all good things that make for self-confident and healthy individuals.

But now ask yourself: Does your job bring out these traits in you, your colleagues, or your boss? Or is it much more likely to bring out things like anxiety, impatience, petulance, authoritarianism, and a pent-up sense of homicidal rage? The contradiction is easy to unpack: the idea that work "builds character" makes sense only outside the context of wage labor, the reality of most people's employment. Sexless Silicon Valley weirdos and horny reptilian politicians alike talk about work as a matter of innate human creativity, self-determination, and boundless possibility. In fact, most jobs chip away at those things until they've been completely annihilated. Jobs *destroy* character, day after miserable day. They drain all the time and energy you would otherwise have for fun, sex, hobbies, and anything other than staring blankly at a computer in the couple of hours you have to yourself after 7:00 p.m.

So when old people tell you that work builds character, what they really mean is that it trains you to slog through hopelessness and alcoholism and to redirect your unexpressed rage toward your family and your loved ones. It doesn't build character, but it sure does build a tolerance to the antidepressants, mood stabilizers, five-hour energy diarrhea drinks, and "focus"-enhancing drugs coursing through your bloodstream.

Another uniquely American lie meant to cover all this up is the idea that "the rich work hardest of all." The premise that the wealthy got that way from working harder than you do—or, at the very least, that they're justly compensated—is a central myth of a country that let a hundred assholes on Wall Street get away with deleting $10 trillion in 2008 and (after brutally suppressing a grassroots "Occupy" movement) immediately pretended it never happened.

Sure, the average CEO or VP *may* work "longer hours" than you, *maybe*, but what are they actually doing with their time? By definition, the only things their job affords them the time to do are pace around their huge office, promote and attend conferences, glaze over during PowerPoint presentations created by other people, trade golf stories over three-martini lunches, and worry about their taxes. The factor of their income over that of a regular person is so astronomical that to be "equal" they would have to work hundreds of times harder and give 10,000 percent all the time. Also: since the 1980s, bosses don't get paid only in terms of salary, they get stock options, too, which are taxed less than income.

As a reward for being a good test taker—or, more likely, for being the child of a good test taker—bosses are compensated at a rate that would shame the Egyptian pharaohs, all in return for "blue-sky thinking" and "inno-vention" that mostly involves putting a marketable gloss on wage theft and parasitic rent-seeking. The average CEO gets paid three hundred times more than you do solely for being the type of creep who impresses imbeciles like David Brooks at Davos.

All right, so maybe they don't toil as hard as their workers, but at least the big bosses do some good by *hiring* all those workers, right?

At one point during the 2016 campaign, Donald Trump called the parents of a fallen US Army officer, Humayun Khan, "so unfair to me, very unfair." In response to this, George Stephanopoulos asked him if he'd ever sacrificed anything in his life comparable to what the Khans and their son had. He responded: "I think I've made a lot of sacrifices. I work very, very hard. I created thousands and thousands of jobs." Pressed to elaborate, he said, "I think those are sacrifices. I think when I can employ thousands and thousands of people, take care of their education, take care of so many things [*sic*]." This quote made headlines for a few hours before being overtaken in the news cycle when Trump claimed, "I fucked Bigfoot. Beautiful! Tremendous!" But it deserves to be remembered.

Of all the off-the-cuff imbecility that Trump spouted during his soggy march toward the White House, this nugget is one of the most revealing bits: How could anyone define the extraction of surplus labor from thousands of people—to fund the construction of Trump's diamond-encrusted sexcopter—as an act of "sacrifice"?

Because, somewhere along the way, a Chamber of Commerce messaging gremlin turned the base metal of capitalist exploitation into the shimmering gold of "job creation." And, because we've torn organized labor to pieces and shipped the shreds to China to be reassembled and shipped back to us as *Emperor's New Groove* Happy Meal toys, there's no one in a position of power to call bullshit on it.

The ugly truth is that no employer hires anyone unless they can extract more value from them than they have to pay out in wages and benefits.

But what about the good ones? "Small businesses"? This fetish is widespread even on the Left. It's nice to think that, far away from the Borg-like monopolies of Wal-Mart and Comcast, there exists a benign, plucky, *authentic* type of business, perhaps run by a cute old Italian couple who employ a bunch of young boys in aprons with slicked-back hair who carry big paper bags of groceries to your doorstep.

If this kind of shop even still exists, it's likely that those slick-haired boys have no stake in the business, have shitty or zero benefits, and are probably huffing vitamins every hour to make it through the day. Little old Giuseppe works everybody till 8:00 p.m., doesn't pay overtime, and has a tendency to pinch all the young women on the hip any chance he gets. Meanwhile, his wife day-drinks and occasionally slips the word *eggplant* into her unnecessary monologues about "urban types" hanging around the neighborhood.

Even more likely, this mythical old couple is actually a loud, crew cut–sporting Trump voter or anti-vaccine Wine Mom who gets away with abusing his or her employees even more than the corporate droids working for Target and McDonalds do. Small-business owners are, generally speaking, insane egomaniacs who believe enough in their "pizza restaurant with a night club atmosphere" to borrow $250,000 and lord it over a workforce of desperate people. And you know what? Even if the boss is a nice person (it can happen), they still deny their employees an equal share in the profits of the business and continue to prop up the completely arbitrary social order that lifts up people with access to a bank loan and makes everyone else dependent on their personal generosity.

The simple fact is, bosses aren't your friends, they're not your parents, and they're not your benefactors. They want to turn your sweat and anxiety and mounting desperation into a second Jet Ski. Asking nicely has never gotten workers anywhere, but that's what people tend to do when they think their boss hired them out of the goodness of his heart. Don't fall for it. The next time you hear "job creator," just imagine your boss sitting on his ass eating a foie gras burrito while you pull a fist-sized ball of pubic hair out of the break room sink.

Work: An Unpaid History

Our modern world runs on pay-by-the-irregular-heartbeat courier apps, "consulting," and financial instruments that will bankrupt pensions if a certain species of bird doesn't go extinct. But it wasn't always like this. To understand how mind-numbingly stupid your job is now, you must first understand the history of the labor economy.

Ancient Times

After humans stopped hunting and gathering for themselves and their immediate families, they started to realize complex needs beyond mere subsistence and rudimentary horniness. Homes needed to be built. Swords needed to be forged. Fucked-up condoms made out of animal bladders that people in the past liked, because they felt natural, needed to be sewn. These ancient occupations were usually centered around necessities, with a smaller portion of jobs devoted to the desires of the wealthy. If you were lucky, you could have been Julius Caesar's foreskin cleaner, King Leonidas's slave trainer, or Hammurabi's coder.

The Middle Ages

After the fall of the Roman Empire, there were some career opportunities in literature and science in places like the Islamic world, the Byzantine Empire, and East Asia. But LinkedIn was hundreds of years away, so people in northern Europe and the scattered remains of the western Roman Empire couldn't relocate to take part in the challenging team-based solutions that made up the burgeoning industries of the East. Instead, they toiled away, creating new, stupid wolf gods for the tribes of the region to worship; bashing rocks into other rocks to create new, exciting shapes; and graffitiing vulgar complaints on abandoned Roman aqueducts in a precursor to the modern Internet comment section.

As civilized kingdoms consolidated their power in Europe, the Saxons, Goths, Visigoths, Ostrogoths, Megagoths, and other assorted tribespeople started to take on even more specialized occupations. For some, that meant translating the Bible into new languages. For others, that meant heaving dead bodies directly into water reservoirs and blaming subsequent deaths on Jewish magic.

But for 99 percent of humanity, this meant being a landless peasant. Serfdom was a full-time job doing backbreaking agricultural labor for a local liege lord, who in turn offered you physical protection from such threats as Saracens, Vikings, and forest berries that turned you gay if you ate them. In fact, until the invention of capitalism, serfdom was the most efficient economic system. It meant full employment and short commutes, as peasants would be helpfully reminded through light dismemberment that they weren't allowed to wander more than ten furlongs away from the hovel where they were born. They spent their entire lives toiling, then died having never found out their last names.

In our modern information economy, we might find this absurd—the idea of a job that requires you to be responsive to your boss's whims at all hours of the week for little to no compensation, forced to adopt officially acceptable political and religious views under threat of termination, and made to live in tiny, dilapidated quarters with total strangers. Indeed, if you're reading this book in your service job's dark, gas-lit breakroom or for a media internship that expects you to blog about how problematic our show is, you're probably wondering how feudal society could have been so backward. But remember that medieval rulers didn't have the benefit of the scientific field of economics that we enjoy today and were thus forced to rely on the augury of court wizards, whose analyses of entrails led them to recommend that a lower tithe rate would spur job growth and ward off the birth of two-headed cattle.

In fourteenth-century England, however, one man rejected the wisdom of the wizards and decided to wander off the road to serfdom. This plucky lowborn, Wat Tyler, led a peasant revolt, spurred on by the words of radical priest John Ball: "When Adam delved and Eve span, who was then the gentleman?" This insistence that it was against God and the notion of equality for the landed aristocracy to exploit the labor of those born into servitude was one of the earliest recorded organized harassment campaigns. The insurgents captured London and sacked several government palaces before the situation was resolved when Tyler and Ball were captured by Richard II's men and mutilated to death, convincing the peasants to return home and agitate for incremental change by working within the system.

The Renaissance

Yes, streets were still paved with human shit, kings were still chosen based on who had the most first cousins for ancestors, and people still thought the devil tricked them into being horny, but the concept of work was starting to resemble its modern incarnation. It took a plague that nearly ended civilization and a series of pointless wars over who was more Catholic, but distinctly nontorturous jobs were beginning to spring up.

Take the day of a typical merchant:

6:00 A.M.: Drink a nice breakfast beverage made of ale, oats, mud, and eggs.

7:00 A.M.: Check up on your daughters to see which one will command the highest market price when she reaches the marrying age of eight.

9:00 A.M.: Trudge your way through the bog-like streets to your establishment, where your perfectly smooth workboy is toiling away at your inventory of leather condoms and selling spices from the Far East that are too spicy for white people, such as salt, and Big Marco Polo–brand pantaloons.

12:30 P.M.: A bird carrying a message from your mistress informs you that your bastard son has inherited your cleft chin.

12:45 P.M.: Outraged, you scream at your smooth workboy to nonspecifically "work harder," ride your horse to the countryside, barge into your mistress's inn, and examine your illegitimate son for facial similarities.

2:00 P.M.: Drink your brunch mead and then make your way back to town.

4:00 P.M.: Arrive back at your establishment and inform the workboy that you're going to meet God.

5:30 P.M.: Trudge home, defeated, and find out three of your seventeen legitimate children have died.

Despite the honor with which such men conducted themselves, there was still a stratosphere of upper-middle-class professions above them. Unlike in today's childproofed, safety-padded world, where it's seen as "cool" to go to the doctor instead of dying of one of several diarrhea-related illnesses, the coolest thing you could be in the Middle Ages was a really tough guy. If you weren't lucky enough to be born a lord, duke, or prince but were absolutely amazing at murdering serfs, you could still be a knight. Knights were the Special-Ops guys of this time, in that they loved gear and functioned as tools for moneyed carriers of syphilis. People thought that was insanely badass, for some reason. Whether it was those storied knights of England, the samurai of Nippon, or the Varangian Guards of Byzantium, every culture at this time had a venerated warrior class. Quite rightfully, no one in those days respected actors or scribes or anyone who could read, so the elite warriors were the real celebrities. But just like the democracy of YouTube now makes celebrity attainable for anyone who can perform cruel and bizarre pranks, the earth was about to open up for the 5 percent of people who didst whatever it tooketh.

As the major nations began expanding their colonial properties, trade between states and continents grew immeasurably. It wasn't a rising tide that lifted all boats, but it *was* a chance to get ahead for people who would do absolutely anything to anybody for a quick buck. If a seafaring sociopath could avoid dying of a funny disease like syphilis or a severe vitamin deficiency, being murdered by his crew, or drowning while attempting to make love to a mermaid, he had the opportunity to return to his homeland for his high school reunion and brag that he'd enslaved thousands, killed millions more through disease, and earned his weight in gold. If one had a genetic susceptibility to diarrhea, there was always the fallback position of intermediary for goods plundered from faraway lands.

The Industrial Revolution

While the sixteenth and seventeenth centuries belonged to slave brokers and codpiece merchants, they were about to get some company. Technological advances in the late seventeenth and eighteenth centuries that were supposed to ease the workload of the poor ended up ramping up their exploitation by making every hour of labor even more ruthlessly efficient. The average peasant may have been illiterate and convinced that his erections controlled the tides, but he knew enough to understand that toiling away in a Dark Satanic Mill sucked ass, so he avoided it. Luckily, the budding capitalist and landowning classes had a foolproof method for creating a motivated, agile workforce: enclosure. That's where you go to a piece of land that had been used for common grazing and foraging for generations, throw a fence around it, and say, "This is mine now." Deprived of their means of subsistence, peasants flocked to cities and filled factory floors, working endlessly to pay for food and lodging that just a few years earlier had been theirs by birthright. This process of dispossession and exploitation was repeated much more brutally for slaves in North America. The lower you were in the labor economy, the more your bosses could squeeze out of you and suck the marrow.

But for the burgeoning middle class and above, life couldn't be better. The wonders of factories, railways, and overall more efficient technology allowed them to acquire wealth while doing very little, and at a greater pace than had ever been seen before. Around this time, the culture of the upper middle class was created. These lucky folks who achieved a decent income needed to differentiate themselves from their mud-drinking forebears, and they did it with the dullest cultural affectations and lamest hobbies possible. They formed a scene that differed from that of the gentry, who entertained themselves with bum fights, "racism orgies," and pederasty.

So, the petite bourgeoisie started eating curiously wet cheeses, seeing plays to make sure they were bad, and babbling endlessly about university wait lists. These things remain the cornerstones of the global upper middle class to this day. Trends such as dog therapy and making one's own bead jewelry may come and go, but the most boring people you know today can trace their intellectual lineage to these middle managers of yore. But if one wasn't incredibly rich, solidly well off, or poor enough to be killed with zero recourse, one had to take a different path. Yes, the lower middle class was relegated to the dumbest occupations yet seen.

After industrialization, a typical lower-middle-class job would be to ride a boat around the world, find rare species of birds, and kill them with your bare hands. The less wanderlust-filled of this type could also slot into occupations like flagpole dancer, iron-lung feces remover, and child catcher. Only the last job is recognizable in today's economy, as it merged with plantation overseer to become what is now known as "police officer." In the later 1800s, these demeaning lower-middle-class jobs dovetailed nicely with colonialism. Colonialism had always existed, but the aforementioned technological and supply-chain advances allowed foreign wealth and labor extraction by rich powers to happen at a previously unimaginable clip. This necessitated a massive presence of officers and their support staff, who were often former bird annihilators and accordion cleaners.

Or, perhaps you were a British colonial officer in India. As an upper-middle-class striver, your true talent came from what you learned by socializing in boarding school. To wit: you may have been charged with overseeing slave labor, working out logistics for mineral interests, and meting out punishment to your colonial subjects, but you actually collected the bulk of your income by looking the other way when your bosses would, say, have a bunch of children pee on their backs while they masturbated. If the colonial underlings were discreet and helpful, they would be rewarded with class mobility.

Today, we can trace accountants, small-business owners, and even the very minor gentry to those imperialist helping hands who could keep a secret a century or two ago. Their descendants don't usually have to witness such rampant murder or sexual psychosis firsthand, however, but instead they must relegate their approval of it. Like many things, the personal touch is lost as time goes on.

The Modern Age

If two features of the premodern world were blaming Jews for plagues and writing long, boring posts, they were about to merge in a new and horrifying way. The late nineteenth and early twentieth centuries featured inconceivably destructive wars, catastrophic economic depressions, and crushing austerity in the face of horrors that seemed to interrupt one another before the first cataclysm had even reached its climax.

With every boom comes a bust, and the modern economy had its fair share. In the olden days, you could lose your job if the species you were skinning went extinct, or you could die because your boss made you drink mercury as part of a science experiment. Once capitalism was in full swing, workers were subject to volatile business cycles, rapid extinction of entire industries, speculation that fucked up the markets, and financialization that frequently cratered the economy and wiped out everyone except for those at the top.

While this may be hard to imagine now in the age of perfect markets, this system chewed up the working class and spit them out, jobless and penniless, while the barons above them profited off the carnage. This new era of industrialization barreled along with more booms and busts than ever before, not to mention the ongoing droughts and famines. In the early twentieth century, the draconian punishment doled out to the losers of World War I combined with the rampant, unregulated vampirism of the upper class led to a global economic calamity that ended up reshaping the world—fascism, Hitler, dance marathons, Fanta, all that stuff.

Finally, as 9/11 fell on December 7, 1941, America entered World War II, and wouldn't you know it, the US actually recovered from the Depression. It turned out that with state control of production and jobs for all, a nation could spend its way out of misery. Of course, this proof of concept of planned economies was instead interpreted as a reason to constantly go to war. Postwar jobs seemed to have been informed by this fact. As the country setting the terms for how the world would look, America could impose a slightly subtler imperialism on the globe than could its Euro-cousins of old. Now those who previously wrote boring screeds on Jews could write about how it was necessary to launch ICBMs at Jamaica to show Cuba we could take a dump on them if we really wanted to.

With the world at America's fingertips, the middle class experienced great upward mobility, buttressed by New Deal and wartime planned-economic policies. A typical workday during the Cold War:

9:00 A.M.: Head into the office.

10:00 A.M.: Tell the only woman who works in your division some weird line like "Your tits could set the sun, Janice," and then have her fired for not acknowledging your cool remark.

11:00 A.M.: Drink seven martinis at a prelunch meeting.

11:30 A.M.: Fall asleep while on the phone with a big account.

11:45 A.M.: Piss yourself.

12:00 P.M.: Drive home to get new pants.

1:00 P.M.: Get distracted because you keep thinking about how hot your mistress's new beehive hairdo is.

1:30 P.M.: Get a five-star hotel room downtown for thirty-five cents.

2:00 P.M.: Have unsatisfying sex during which you don't finish because you're shitfaced.

10:00 P.M.: Drive home to find your wife already passed out on Valium.

10:30 P.M.: Try to tuck your kids in with a bedtime story but end up in tears as you tell a weird tale from your childhood about how your mom made you wear a sailor outfit until you were twelve and your uncles hit you on your ass with parade batons to "de-sissify" you.

11:00 P.M.: Fall asleep under the coffee table.

9:00 A.M., Next Day: Show up to work in the exact same clothes you wore yesterday and get a promotion to VP of Big Accounts, because it turns out you and your boss's boss served in the same Navy unit during the war. You now make a handsome salary of $2,500 a year ($1.7 million in 2018 money).

Not a bad deal, if you were white and male and aged twenty-five to eighty-five. But everything must come to an end. As the West deindustrialized and production moved to places where factories could still kill a bunch of people, blue-collar workers began making less and less as their wages were adjusted for changes in the Consumer Price Index. Loads of manufacturing processes were automated, resulting in fewer and fewer decent-paying jobs for the working class that supported the lifestyles of heroic, alcoholic, predatory middle managers. Ignoring the contradictions of capital and labor suddenly wasn't so easy.

That was, until someone had a revolutionary idea: What if a bunch of numbers were displayed on a computer, arbitrarily assigned value, and traded back and forth?

As American manufacturing and commerce shriveled and died, the finance industry slammed a needle full of adrenaline into the puffy chest of the capitalist class. Before the late 1970s, if you wanted to do cocaine, perpetrate sex crimes, and generally make the world worse, you had to work in film or TV production, and that industry had an incredibly high barrier of entry. In finance, however, you could rule the eighties and be as evil as you wanted to be, so long as you abandoned most of your friends and principles, attended an elite university, and were willing to jack off onto a skeleton or whatever people do to get into a Harvard dining club.

Imaginary money exploded everywhere as the Right took a hatchet to hard-won pension programs and worker protections. With rivers of cheap cash flowing like Bawls at a LAN party, new, even dumber jobs could now be created. Before, one may have been a mechanic or worked in an auto plant. But with loose, runny capital spraying everywhere, made-up professions like "marketing director" and "creative consultant" sprang up. Blue-collar wages lagged far behind CPI adjusted for inflation, but a college degree and adequate connections still allowed you to take a job you loved, if you loved truly stupid shit.

If the age of financialization midwifed a dumb new era of work, the tech boom nurtured it into an awkward, cruel, and greedy child. The Internet, at one time a DARPA project that hosted communities of recluses who argued about locking mechanisms and *The Rockford Files*, became a service everyone used. This inaugurated what became known as the "Information Age." Because we were used to overvaluing things based on what the stimulant-addled only children in finance said, we took a deep breath and declared AOL to be worth, like, $500 billion and that Pets.com would found a moon colony.

The party came to a stop when everyone finally realized that 98 percent of those Internet firms didn't generate any revenue, but a lumpy crew of sociopaths got in and got out with expert timing.

Job Interview Tips and Tricks

Jobs. We all need them, but how does one obtain one? It's a lengthy and debasing process, eventually resolved only by knowing someone who knows someone who already has one. Here are a few tricks of the trade to help you land your dream gig!

- **Answer every question with another question. For instance, if the interviewer asks something like, "What unique skills will you bring to this position?" answer, "What skills don't I have?" If they seek further clarification with something like "Name a few" or "I'm asking you," just keep turning the tables by repeating back some variation of their question. "How can I name a few?" or "Who's conducting this interview, you or me?" (even though it's them). This will show that you are confident and motivated.**
- **Never flatly say no to any question. Always respond with "Yes, and . . ." to advance the bit and keep open any possible avenue of inquiry and action.**
- **The person interviewing you is courted by people like you all day. They're used to being complimented and flattered. Throw them off balance and take control of the interaction by doing the opposite and subtly insulting them to undermine their confidence. For example: "That's a nice watercooler; I've seen the same one at every other office I've been to."**
- **Dress conservatively, but add at least one piece of flair to set you apart: a captain's hat, a single leather glove, goggles, or a Renaissance-style carnival mask and cape.**
- **Many employers will now check up on your social media presence during the hiring process, so make sure you've posted a lot of quality content. If you don't have any good content, create a dummy account and fill it with motivational success memes about how "Every stone they throw at you is another brick in your castle" and "A lion is a king of the jungle but still needs a queen." Make sure to reference memes you saw online and thought were funny during the actual face-to-face interview.**
- **Do ask to use the bathroom during the interview even if you don't have to go. Don't accept any beverage offered; it's a sign of weakness.**

Guys like Marc Andreessen, Peter Thiel, and Elon Musk sold their grossly overvalued stakes in computer crap for nerds, walked away with billions, and were able to transform Silicon Valley from a community of weird garages to a speculator's paradise, where men in quarter-zip sweaters shuffle around ten-figure capital allocations in between blogging about sea barges where ephebophilia is legal.

That about catches us up to today.

Tomorrow's Exploitation Today!

The survivors of the dot-com bubble have created an economy so fucking stupid that it's practically one of those Old Testament stories in which a bunch of assholes try to build a tower that will allow them to touch the face of YHWH and receive an ironic punishment from God. It's as if the people who witnessed Hiroshima and escaped safely returned to the same place and built their houses out of yellowcake uranium and played weekly games of dynamite toss.

Yes, the jobs of the future are generated by the incel kingdom of Silicon Valley, where man-children force feed you a subsistence gruel while you slave harder to invent a blood-testing device that streams your results to a chat room of asshole doctors before completely draining the rest of your body. You're doing something very noble, and that's why your boss cashed out to the tune of a few hundred million and you have to sublet your closet. The last tech guy who spoke with such flair about his vision for humanity was Steve Jobs, and he died because he decided to cure his pancreatic cancer by drinking smoothies and doing male power kegels. You can kill a man but not his ideas, and so years after Jobs's demise every single one of his fellow tech lords fancies themselves a "visionary" or "explorer," words previously reserved for Leonardo da Vinci or Magellan rather than someone who gets VC money for inventing a Wi-Fi–enabled box that will keep all your food cold so it doesn't go bad.

The present and future of work is a lot like its past: stupid and arbitrary, and everyone's terrible boss gets to fail upward to the next thing he can fuck up. These days, most jobs are positions that used to be done by five different people, squeezing out every last drop of labor with more hours, more intensity, and more productivity. You receive the privileges of e-mailing people who have sublimated their personality disorders into "management styles" and playing the pawn in bizarre office power plays between proud MBAs. And you're lucky to do it.

Since a large part of Western manufacturing sectors have been moved to countries where factory owners receive tax credits for each worker killed in building collapses, the economy has seen a lot of change in the past forty years. The two people you, the reader, know with steady jobs are most likely in one of the following businesses.

Jobs You Will Probably Never Have

Marketing

If we think of today's horrifying, depersonalizing, and culture-obliterating jobs as a kind of military hierarchy, marketing would be the Green Berets. Like their Army counterparts, marketing professionals are scary because they're not just doing this to pay off student loans—they legitimately enjoy their work and think it's important. Advertising and marketing gigs make up one-sixth of all jobs in America, and if our nation continues to eat its own economic droppings, this figure will likely keep growing. The typical marketing professional is named something like Jordan Adam Taylor, posts things like "Can't relate to dreading Monday because my job just plain rocks #playhardatwork," and is dedicated to brand synergy whether they're asleep, awake, mid-coitus, giving birth, or dead.

Finance

Finance is even more harmful to the world than marketing, but members of this industry don't labor under the delusion that they're fun people who make a difference. A Wall Street guy's work life is a dull affair enlivened only by sporadic STD scares, drug withdrawals, and market panics caused by his own actions—but mostly it's just staring at screens as numbers jump around and increase his wealth by three sets of commas at a time.

Investment banks and trading-house hiring departments look for distinct characteristics in potential employees—bedwetting well into puberty, animal torture during adolescence, all the Dark Triad/ Six Sigma personality trait clusters. If you love variable-interest-rate mortgages and creating value for the grandchildren of Nazi war profiteers, finance is for you.

Law Enforcement

If you've woken up every day of your life and decided that your rage issues and utter fear of anything that doesn't look like you should dictate who lives or dies, it may be time for your Blue Life to matter.

After all, cops are workers, just like anyone else. Yes, they'll stave in your skull if you organize for a union, but they also head outside every day, see a meme with an unattributed quote from Kanye saying that rapping is harder than being a cop, write utterly moronic open letters steeped in self-pity despite having a less dangerous job than crab fishermen, and then spend the rest of the day playing with the repurposed Stinger missiles that the federal government gave their department.

Academia

Once the highest pursuit among naked Greek men, the scholarly professions are now all about getting tenure, doing safe spaces, and getting triggered by logic. Generations ago, professors were honorable people. There were science professors who would see a sexy lady and knock beakers and scales off their desks with their nerd boners; old-money classicists who could recite the words of any number of ancient sex perverts while blackout drunk on a boat; idealistic English professors who had yet to make their turn to the right and founded *The Journal of Western Greatness* after the campus PC-police and feminazis made their students stop sleeping with them; and dispassionate economic scholars who weren't afraid to take money from United Fruit Co. to report that people in other countries actually enjoy de facto slavery.

Now, however, academia is a Ponzi scheme with beer pong, a soulless grind where you're expected to turn out long, boring papers called, like, "Fear of Castration and the Western Male Explored through Reggaeton" or face summary execution by the dean. Every year, thousands of freshly minted PhDs compete for a handful of tenure-track jobs, surviving off adjunct appointments and pilfered cafeteria lunch meat. Most of them will burn out and attempt to enter the private job market, which will have no use for anyone who spent a decade studying gnostic imagery in the films of Pauly Shore. The lucky few will hang on long enough to inherit the Distinguished Chair in Kanye Studies at Devilstick University.

If you think you have it in you to talk and write endlessly about subjects you barely know anything about for a bunch of slack-jawed early-twenties layabouts with no prospects, give it a shot, but we can't imagine living our lives that way.

Jobs You Probably *Will* Have

Now, if you're a fan of ours, the aforementioned jobs will belong to your more successful friends and nonfail siblings. You, dear reader, are more likely to slot into these exciting careers:

Service

Join your peers in retail or food and beverage, where the worst middle-class authoritarians scan your restaurant or store for anything that upsets them so they can scream at you. These are people who've never been mad for a legitimate reason, but they love the feeling. You just have to stare at their disgusting wet maws flapping around until they hit a fever pitch and jet cum down their hideous pale legs. Whether it's a server position at a restaurant, a footwear salesman who must shoo away enterprising perverts, or customer service for a telecom giant whose favorability polls are lower than the Islamic State's, you'll witness every fucked-up power trip that those who have never held any authority but have long fantasized about abusing it take.

Since there are barely any job protections anymore, a service employee almost always has to submit to the demands of suburban sociopaths. Does a lawyer with a teetering marriage and a clown-core dubstep DJ son who doesn't respect him want lobster even though he's at a burger chain? Better locate the nearest seafood wholesaler, or at least hope his taste buds are too fried by SSRIs to detect imitation crabmeat. Is a man older than dirt telling you "I'd love to see a smile and something else on that face?" He knows that the restaurant can pay you slave wages if you're a tipped employee, and he's wagering you're not gonna make a fuss, given that he's from a different generation and all.

Content Creation

You may think you want this job. You may think you can do it. But 99.9 percent of the time, people who emerge as triumphant heroes from the content mines end up with AdSense lung, broken spirits, and empty pockets. Content—be it a think piece, a call-out tweet, or something really degenerate, like a podcast—is one of the only real, tangible products we make anymore. But its creation also puts more physical and mental demands on workers than the most grizzled military operators have to endure. In a sense, content makers are more troop-like than troops themselves, as information is the battlefield of the twenty-first century.

If you really think you're ready to answer a bunch of awful, piggish fans and find new ways to say someone you're making fun of is ugly every day, go for it. But don't say we didn't warn you.

Serfdom

You could be run ragged driving for a ride-sharing app created by a company that loses about $535 billion a month while still retaining a $900 billion valuation, until the shifty worm who founded the business is recorded doing his Benny Hill impression in the boardroom, writes a weepy open letter promising to do better, and leaves the company.

Camming

A new frontier of sex work that doesn't involve leaving the house, "camming" is the fastest-growing sector of employment for the millennial precariat. Camming refers to the webcam that will broadcast you masturbating, and if you already spend much of the day lying prone in bed, laptop on your stomach, staring into the void of online social interaction, then you're already halfway there. Jacking off is a fun hobby that anyone can do, and now it's one you can get paid for.

If you're willing to jack off with friends positioned at awkward angles to fill a computer screen, then, friend, you're now a Web entrepreneur! However, if spending all day responding to comments like "want to see the titty, so sexxy :)," "get that fucking cat out of the way," or "need natural uncut for space dock!" from anonymous users is not your cup of tea, then you might consider camming-adjacent activities like eating lots of food or whispering.

Presidential Tweet Replier

The collapse of American political discourse into a frenzied Internet shouting festival has been disastrous for the country, but it could be a boon to your bank account! Having a president who uses his toilet time to yell on social media means there's a huge captive audience for the dedicated Twitter influencer who can reply instantly each time the president tweets "Lying media says I never fucked Sandy Duncan. FAKE NEWS! She gave me a hand job at the *Mac and Me* premiere!"

With millions of people engaging with the replies attached to the bottom of a presidential tweet, the potential for lucrative self-promotion is limitless. If you're a nebulously credentialed verified account holder who's sick of the president's disgusting behavior, you can parlay typing "Sir, how DARE you!" into a crowdfunded podcast in which you lay out just how the KGB funded the career of Larry the Cable Guy. Or, if you're of the other political persuasion and can program a bot to respond to those tweets with patriotic memes in which troops cry because of hip-hop, then you can make a mint selling coffee mugs that say "Liberal Cum" and "My Other Coffee Cup is a Gun."

But, you may be asking, what if we eventually reach a point where we *don't* have a head of state who live-tweets his mental decline? Luckily, that's never going to happen. We've entered the Aeon of Horus. Nothing is true. Everything is permitted. And the president will, from now until the sun gutters out, be a megalomaniacal Internet addict. So start practicing your "I wish Malcolm was still in the Middle and not on the Extreme Right" burns for when President Frankie Muniz starts deporting redheads.

Bio Bag

"Sell yourself," they told you. In a fast-paced, ever-changing knowledge economy, getting ahead means making yourself indispensable. Hustling, schmoozing, and self-promoting that internship into a job offer or that freelance gig into a staff position. But in a future when automation will render a huge proportion of human labor input superfluous, "sell yourself" is going to take on a more literal meaning. If all you have to sell is your labor and nobody is buying, your only remaining commodities are your blood, sperm/eggs, and organs, which the failing bodies of the ruling class will always have use for. Shaving off a quarter of your liver every six months may sound traumatic, but it beats being picked up in a Loiter Sweep and having all your blood pressed out of your body like a toothpaste tube and used for vampire cosplay by Peter Thiel.

A New Life Awaits You in the Facebook Colonies

The final cliché meant to keep you on board our system's sinking ship is that work is *fun*, that your office has foosball, that pizza is delivered on Friday, and that your boss rides a hoverboard. It's not really a job as much as a quirky, cool place you never have to leave. Originally associated with Silicon Valley techno-utopias (Facebook is now building Wi-Fi gulags that allow workers to eat, shower, and sleep at the office),* the idea has now metastasized throughout

* Avery Hartmans, "Facebook Is Building a Village That Will Include Housing, a Grocery Store and a Hotel," *Business Insider*, July 7, 2017.

much of our culture. Some ghoulish app company runs a subway ad campaign with slogans such as "You Eat Coffee for Lunch" and "Sleep Deprivation Is Your Drug of Choice." That's real.

In other words, for a certain cohort of young, white-collar drones, the modern workplace has become a giant, countrywide adult day care center. Of course, those working blue-collar and service jobs will still be subjected to good old-fashioned Panopticon surveillance, but as automation starts to "professionalize" those jobs or simply kill them and drive their workers into the freelance gig economy, the triumph of this Silicon Valley nanovirus seems inevitable.

The expectation that the office should also be the center of your social life, that one need never leave to enjoy activities usually associated with "free time," is perhaps the most insidious idea about work yet devised. This is the final frontier, the newest batshit notion the ruling class wants to normalize the way it normalized privatized health care, extraction of surplus labor, and thanking your boss for not letting you die in the street. It's a new, futuristic, permanent utopia where *your job and your free time are the same thing.* It's a complete, perverse inversion of the socialist or communist idea, the alternative vision. One we should probably get around to describing now . . .

When freed from the soul-crushing system of wage labor, what we used to call "work" actually becomes the passionate, creative fulfillment the lizards in marketing tell us it is. After setting everyone on equal footing (by seizing the billionaires' money, socializing their wealth, and handing the keys to production over to workers), you're looking at an economy that requires something like a three-hour workday, with machines taking care of most of the drudgery; and—as our public fund pays for things like health care, education, scientific research, and infrastructure—all this technology *actually* makes work quicker, easier, and more enjoyable.

It Will Set You Free

But right now, the gap between the promise of technology and the actually existing, deeply stupid reality couldn't be more obvious. Instead of a means to liberate you, technology is a tool for your boss to track you, message you, and harass you at any time of day, whether you're on the clock or not. It doesn't enhance your free time, it destroys it. It has you checking your phone, e-mail, or Slack feed every three hundred seconds while you're awake, and, once the next generation of iPhone rolls out, during your REM sleep as well. Meanwhile, the same people preaching the gospel of "innovation"—the Cory Bookers and Paul Ryans both—are scheming to privatize every last facet of your life, grooming everyone born after 1980 to work, work, work until they all keel over.

The supposed trade-off, of course, is that the more you work, the more stuff you get. There was a commercial a couple of years back featuring the blond guy from *Band of Brothers* in which he owns France for taking two-month vacations, bragging that, in America, we take just *two weeks* off and *earn* the money to buy a Lexus instead. He walks into his McMansion with his hot wife—and so can you.

Except this is also a lie. There is no Lexus, no McMansion, and no gold-encrusted bidet waiting for you, no matter how hard you work. Thanks to an unrelenting class war waged since about 1973, wages have stayed the same for four decades, while money has been funneled to the top. Even supposed nest eggs like 401ks and pensions are wired to the insane, wealth-obliterating machine of the stock market, which can and will implode again and again.

And if we manage to get across one thing in this stupid book, let it be this: it doesn't have to be this way. Even weak-ass, social-democratic France passed a law a couple of years ago making it illegal for companies with more than fifty employees to hound staff after hours, and no matter how hard neoliberal pod-person Emmanuel Macron tries, he can't seem to pry the country's labor code out of the hands of the citizens who like it. It's why a century ago, even the assholes who *liked* the system didn't think it would last this long: in the 1920s, John Maynard Keynes was predicting that we would have a twenty-hour workweek by now. America itself was on this road in the twentieth century, slicing down the workweek, granting labor rights, and taking care of all the shit your paycheck had to cover. The tragedy of the 1970s wasn't that the cycle was broken but that it simply started over.

So don't believe the tech lizards, the reactionary billionaires, or the Democratic paypigs who tell you that work is actually cool. It won't be cool until their bank accounts are emptied into everyone else's and "work" becomes something you squeeze in between posting, gaming, and having a nice, big wank.

EPILOGUE

"My father always told me . . .
He said when you think you've done all you can do
and you think you can't do no more . . . do some more."

—Steve Harvey

Absorbing the litany of horrors committed in American history by both Knuckle-Dragging Conservatives™ and Well-Meaning Liberals™, a reader might be compelled to call us on our shit and demand, "Okay, assholes, but where was the Left during all of this?"

Besides doing the grassroots organizing and agitating that pushed those Well-Meaning Liberals™ into backing social and economic reforms, the answer is: getting shot, arrested, deported, spied on, and purged. Since socialists, Marxists, and left-wingers of all stripes were the only people challenging the hegemony of capitalism in America, they were targeted for harassment, intimidation, and death at all turns. The list of left-wing martyrs destroyed by state and right-wing vigilante violence reads like a who's-who of activists in the labor and civil rights movements, from Albert Parsons to MLK. The strongest, smartest activists for justice in this country did not seek to "reform" capitalism and its hierarchy but to destroy it—so capitalism and its hierarchy destroyed them first.

Under that pressure, the Left cracked. Driven from the ranks of increasingly business-friendly labor unions and with its political parties shot through with informants and provocateurs, the movement splintered into microsects and retreated into the ivory tower of academia (from which the Marxists were eventually also purged).

However, this neo–Gilded Age is creating wealth disparity and precariousness that have millions of Americans questioning the underlying logic of capitalism in a way that hasn't happened in generations. Lefties are again at the tip of the spear against a desperate capitalist system that's readying a blood-soaked, militarized response to climate and economic catastrophes.

And believe us, those catastrophes are coming. You don't have to be a mindset genius to realize that the engine of capital, running on greed and the vampiric logic of profit, will fuck up the world over and over again. Who knows what will happen first: A new speculative bubble that obliterates people's wealth as it enriches an ever-ascendant class of inbred oligarchs? A final wave of automation that destroys everyone's job, leaving no one left to buy anything and crashing the economy? Or the first singular 100,000-plus-death-toll climate event caused by decades of thrashing the planet for profit?

Of course, there's a chance that a natural extinction event like a supervolcano or meteor will wipe out all human life, letting capitalism off the hook. But barring that merciful possibility, the parasitic system that runs our world will 100 percent, for sure, you betcha end up ruining or killing at least one person you know in your lifetime.

That is, unless we finally stun the beast, reach for the cattle gun, and scoop its brains out; unless we find a moment or series of moments to claw back power from the Jeff Bezoses and Bill Gateses and Charles Kochs, whose wealth could instantly end world poverty four times over.

Finding some happiness in this hellworld is essential for your mental health, but it's not enough. No one would blame you for simply "getting by"—zoning out after work, ordering the occasional GrubHub delivery, and saving up for a PS4. But you'll still feel the dread. Fact is, there's no way to truly escape the anxiety and alienation, let alone the economic and ecological catastrophes we're going to witness in our lifetimes.

Getting by is not enough. But neither is ceaseless anger, sadness, and fear. That will burn you out quickly, and what you need is energy to sustain you, to motivate you to be a part of something bigger. Spending every single moment thinking about politics (particularly on the Internet) will turn you cynical, hysterical, and probably reactionary. Let's avoid that.

What we all need—as far as our ancient, wise, giant brains can tell—is a good-humored, thick-skinned, and maybe even optimistic struggle against the world outside. You may be thinking that that's easy for *us* to say, since we've stumbled onto some success and money for our very dumb but also very brilliant comedy show. But the truth is, we really did believe this stuff when we were broke, and we'll believe it a year from now after we foolishly invest all our money in BitcoinDark and lose everything.

It's true—we don't know much. But we know this: as the liberal opposition to Trump (and whatever nightmare comes after Trump) reveals itself to be feckless and incompetent, more and more people are going to realize that there is no reforming a system built on exploitation and nonstop, infinite economic growth. Socialism will emerge as the only genuine alternative to the savage, hopeless, gangster system of capitalism—an alternative that offers an actual future, one in which there are enough resources to take care of everybody and to take on humanity's challenges with a dab of dignity.

That, or we'll all drown in boiling seawater. Always good to have options.

ACKNOWLEDGMENTS

In the course of writing this book, a number of people have provided us with insight, moral support, hugs, and faves. Tradition dictates that we recognize them at the end of the text, despite the fact that we wrote it and they just kind of existed in our orbit while we were doing the real work. If we are the sun lighting up this project's solar system and supporting all life, the following are a few of the lifeless rocks and gas clouds that have coalesced around us.

First and foremost, for making this book possible, we thank our editor, Matthew Benjamin; Lara Blackman, Abigail Novak, and the whole team at Touchstone. We'd also like to recognize our literary agent, Daniel Greenberg, for bringing this prize hog to the county fair.

Outside the immediate business of books, we'd like to thank our managers, Ben Curtis and Parker Oks, for their dedication to our inane pursuits; Brett Pain and Bryan Quinby of *Street Fight Radio* for being our podcast godfathers; James Adomian for his brilliant and unique contributions to the show; Eli Valley and Jon White for their amazing artwork; our producer, Chris Wade, for his heroic work in making us listenable; and the staff of Nostrand Café, who let us drive away most of their customers while we spent hours at their workplace writing this book and drinking from the same smoothie with five straws.

We'd now like to break from the collective and each individually acknowledge the people who weaned us on the milk of their virtue and character.

Will: More than anything I want to thank the haters, trolls, and everyone who is mad for making this all possible. Special thanks to Robert Weil and all my former colleagues at Liveright and W.W. Norton for giving me my first real job and teaching me everything I know about books. Also much love to my cohosts and coauthors who made writing this book so damn fun. Thank you to Marty for finding me, and to Katherine for keeping me. Finally, and of least importance to my success, I'd like to acknowledge Katherine Bouton, Daniel Menaker, and Lizi Menaker—that's my mom, dad, and sister to you goofies. In the words of Ricky Henderson, "Today I am the greatest of all time, thank you."

Brendan: For inspiring my contributions to this book and my creative pursuits in general, a sincere thank-you to Dave Hackel and Tim Berry, the creators and producers of the underrated and oft-maligned sitcom *Becker* (1998–2004). Set in the New York City borough of the Bronx, the show starred Ted Danson as John Becker, a misanthropic doctor who operates a small practice and is constantly annoyed by his patients, coworkers, friends, and practically everything and everybody else in his world. Despite everything, his patients and friends are loyal because Becker genuinely cares about them.

Virgil: This book would never have existed had it not been for my old editor, Blake Zeff, who introduced us to Daniel Greenberg to pitch another, less extant book. Thank you to everyone over the years who faved and RTed and made this go viral. Thank you to the celebs. And thank you to Blair, to whom I dedicate the good parts of this book.

Felix: Mom, Sam, Lucy: I did it. To my grandmother: I also did it. To my friends Brandon, Kyle, Jalil: Call me Steven King, because I made it. Special thanks to the Hudson boys for the Stephen King joke. Listen to the Episode 1 podcast. Piece!

Matt: Thanks to my mother, Jo Ann, my stepfather, Glenn, my sister, Sarah, and to my wife (borat), Carolyn, eternal love and gratitude.

GRIEVANCES

While we join most authors in providing an acknowledgments section, we feel it is just as important to recognize those who antagonized us, held us back, and stood opposed to our mission.

In no particular order: Mr. Bloss, ninth-grade math teacher who said we would never be able to make a podcast; Ashleigh, that barista who never smiles; Leon Trotsky, terrorist and hound of fascism; The *New York Times* editorial board; The *Washington Post* editorial board; the *IGN* editorial board; actor Benedict Cumberbatch; Boss Burger on Ave U in Washington, DC; the entire city of Washington, DC; all of the incredibly minor inconveniences that have made Felix want to kill himself; every listener or fan who has approached us with so-called "constructive criticism"; the dead—everyone who has ever died and whose psychic weight bears down on the nightmare of history like the grave itself; and finally, all mods, especially Darth_Ayatollah88, who arbitrarily banned us from the GameFAQs off-topic message board on September 17, 2004, for daring to question the rationale behind male circumcision.

UH, SOURCES FOR THESE CLAIMS?

You should believe everything we say without asking for "evidence." However, in the event that you would like to look up some of the more surprising tidbits—or the embarrassing things written and said by our enemies—we've provided footnotes throughout and a brief bibliography below.

Chapter One

Harvey, David. *Marx, Capital, and the Madness of Economic Reason*. New York: Oxford University Press, 2018.

Jones, Jeffrey M. "Blacks Showing Decided Opposition to War." *Gallup*, March 28, 2003. http://news.gallup.com/poll/8080/blacks-showing-decided-opposition-war.aspx.

Chapter Two

Applebome, Peter. "Death Penalty; Arkansas Execution Raises Questions on Governor's Politics." *New York Times*, January 25, 1992. http://www.nytimes.com/1992/01/25/us/1992-campaign-death-penalty-arkansas-execution-raises-questions-governor-s.html.

Caro, Robert A. *Master of the Senate: The Years of Lyndon Johnson*. New York: Vintage Books, 2003.

Clinton, Hillary. *It Takes a Village*. New York: Simon & Schuster, 1996.

Cowie, Jefferson. *Stayin' Alive: The 1970s and the Last Days of the Working Class.* New York: New Press, 2010.

Freeman, Joshua B. *Working-Class New York: Life and Labor Since World War II.* New York: New Press, 2001.

Royko, Mike. "Ok, So 'Trailer Trash' and 'Democrat' Not Always the Same." *South Florida SunSentinel,* January 29, 1997. http://articles.sun-sentinel.com/1997-01-29/news/9701270210_1_paula-jones-trailer-park-trailer-trash.

Weigant, Chris. "A New Direction for America?" *Huffington Post,* June 23, 2006. https://www.huffingtonpost.com/chris-weigant/a-new-direction-for-ameri_b_23684.html.

Chapter Three

Clines, Francis X. "Appearing Nightly: Robert Dornan, Master of the Put-Down." *New York Times,* June 27, 1995. http://www.nytimes.com/1995/06/27/us/appearing-nightly-robert-dornan-master-of-the-put-down.html.

Dionne, E. J., Jr. "Is Buchanan Courting Bias?" *Washington Post,* February 29, 1992. https://www.washingtonpost.com/archive/politics/1992/02/29/is-buchanan-courting-bias/4753a57f-183b-4033-be38-4e2360e6aa00/.

Hoppe, Hans-Hermann. *Democracy—The God That Failed: The Economics and Politics of Monarchy, Democracy, and Natural Order.* New Brunswick, NJ: Transaction Publishers, 2001.

Martin, Jonathan, and Amie Parnes. "McCain: Obama Not an Arab, Crowd Boos." *Politico*, October 10, 2008. https://www.politico.com/story/2008/10/mccain-obama-not-an-arab-crowd-boos-014479.

Rand, Ayn. "Screen Guide for Americans." The Motion Picture Alliance for the Preservation of American Ideals, 1947. http://archive.lib.msu.edu/DMC/AmRad/screenguideamericans.pdf.

Solomon, Deborah. "Of Manliness and Men." *New York Times Magazine*, March 12, 2006. http://www.nytimes.com/2006/03/12/magazine/of-manliness-and-men.html.

Chapter Four

Dee, Jonathan. "Right-Wing Flame War!" *New York Times Magazine*, January 21, 2010. http://www.nytimes.com/2010/01/24/magazine/24Footballs-t.html.

"Fact Check: Johnson's 'Saint Pancake' Comment Stood for Years." *Diary of Daedalus* (blog). December 7, 2011. https://thediaryofdaedalus.com/2011/12/07/fact-check-johnsons-saint-pancake-comment-stood-for-years/.

Klein, Ezra. "Bernie Sanders's Single-Payer Plan Isn't a Plan at All." *Vox*, January 17, 2016. https://www.vox.com/2016/1/17/10784528/bernie-sanders-single-payer-health-care.

———. "The Health of Nations." *American Prospect*, April 22, 2007. http://prospect.org/article/health-nations.

———. "Mistakes, Excuses and Painful Lessons from the Iraq War." *Bloomberg View*, March 19, 2013. https://www.bloomberg.com/view/articles/2013-03-19/mistakes-excuses-and-painful-lessons-from-the-iraq-war.

McArdle, Megan. "Bring It On." *Asymmetrical Information*, February 13, 2003. https://archive.is/Yitep.

———. "How Much Is the War Going to Cost?" *Asymmetrical Information*, March 23, 2003. https://archive.is/GSvUm.

———. "A Really, Really, Really Long Post about Gay Marriage That Does Not, in the End, Support One Side or the Other." *Asymmetrical Information*, April 2, 2005. http://archive.today/DL3ja.

———. "There's Little We Can Do to Prevent Another Massacre." *Daily Beast*, December 17, 2012. https://www.thedailybeast.com/theres-little-we-can-do-to-prevent-another-massacre.

Moulitsas, Markos. "Be Happy for Coal Miners Losing Their Health Insurance. They're Getting Exactly What They Voted For." *Daily Kos*, December 12, 2016. https://www.dailykos.com/stories/2016/12/12/1610198/-Be-happy-for-coal-miners-losing-their-health-insurance-They-re-getting-exactly-what-they-voted-for.

Smith, Ben. "My Life in the Blogosphere." *BuzzFeed*, January 28, 2015. https://www.buzzfeed.com/bensmith/this-is-my-blog?utm_term=.ufPmlmOWb#.ghlvQv9mY.

Sullivan, Andrew. "ABC News' John Miller Likens Bin Laden to Teddy Roosevelt." *Daily Dish*, September 19,

2001. http://dish.andrewsullivan.com/2001/09/19/abc-news-john-miller-likens-bin-laden-to-teddy-roosevelt/.

———. "Today." *Daily Dish,* September 11, 2001. http://dish.andrewsullivan.com/2001/09/11/today-4/.

Yglesias, Matthew. "Different Places Have Different Safety Rules and That's OK." *Slate,* April 24, 2014. http://www.slate.com/blogs/moneybox/2013/04/24/international_factory_safety.html.

Chapter Five

No facts were required.

Chapter Six

Hartmans, Avery. "Facebook Is Building a Village That Will Include Housing, a Grocery Store and a Hotel." *Business Insider,* July 7, 2017. http://www.businessinsider.com/facebook-building-employee-housing-silicon-valley-headquarters-2017-7.

INDEX

ABOUT THE AUTHORS

Felix Biederman is a member of the PlayStation Network, a fellow at Xbox Live, and professor emeritus at Steam. He is the author of the espionage thrillers *The Husband's Wife, Wifeocracy, The Wife Cuts Both Ways,* and *The Backgammon Deception,* as well as the hard sci-fi novella *Chronicles Of J'ariska: Origins.*

Matt Christman is a humorist and raconteur with a lifelong love of broadcasting, political comedy, and exploring shipwrecks for sunken treasure. As part of *Chapo Trap House,* Matt has recorded hundreds of hours of podcast content, performed more than a dozen live shows, and salvaged long-lost galleons and frigates from the Spanish Main to the Barbary Coast. He lives in a crow's nest made of melted pieces of eight.

Brendan James is a writer, musician, and ~~producer emeritus~~ traitor of *Chapo Trap House.* An early member of the show, his revisionist tendencies and collusion with cosmopolitan elements of foreign podcasts resulted in his forced expulsion in 2017. Since then, a loose network of his so-called Jacobite followers have spread lies and terror among the peace-loving *Chapo* fanbase on Reddit, Discord, and Friendster. From exile, James continues to disseminate toxic propaganda in his newsletter, *The Masked Merovingian,* where he demands the show return to the .wav format. His lies have also appeared in *The Baffler, Newsweek, Deadspin, Vice,* the *Guardian,* and *Slate.*

Will Menaker is a publishing industry scion who grew up on the Upper West Side of Manhattan as the product of a secret KGB/FBI breeding program to produce a star child capable of sheep-dogging gullible millennials into supporting reformistpettybougimperialismamerikkka and/or tanking the 2016 election for Donald Trump. He is the creator of the "Menaker Mindset" motivational success brand and the editor of many prize-winning and bestselling books and graphic novels such as: *Booger-Eater: A Memoir, Garfield Dungeon: The Best of DeviantArt, The Cardassian Gambit: A DS9 Novelization, Generation Selfie, Invisible Battleground: A Mason Tank Novel,* and *The Glass Chickadee: Poems.* He lives in Brooklyn.

Virgil Texas is a satirist whose yuks and sends-up have tickled readers' funny bones everywhere from the *Toast* ("If Caddy Compson Were On Tinder It Would Go A Little Something Like This") to *McSweeney's* ("Carmen Sandiego Tries To Find Nambia") to the *New Yorker,* where he authors the popular column "Borowitz Report." His quips have had the public rolling in bookstore aisles from coast to coast with such recent titles as *Grab 'Em By the Debussy: Classical Song Parodies for the #Resistance*; *Nevertheless, She Exfoliated: The Nasty Woman's Self Care-a-Day Desk Calendar for Keeping Sane in the Age of Drumpf*; and *Make America Snark Again: A Covfefe Table Book* (with forward by Ken Bone). He can be found three nights a week at the Allen Dulles Theatre in Washington, DC, performing with his band the Capitol Steps (tickets available through Ticketmaster).